Foreword by
Don Piper

Heaven

From Victim
to Victory

A Story of Hope

Brian †Arnold

America's Favorite One-Handed Pianist

Endorsements

I'm so happy Brian has written this book. His story is an amazing one and I know it will be a blessing and encouragement to so many others. God has brought him through so much, as you will see in these pages. Brian shares his life openly and I know you will see God's hand on him through his entire journey. Sometimes we forget that God is always with us and even when we aren't walking as we should He is there because He knows the plans He has for us. Our Savior uses all kinds of experiences to mold and shape us into becoming people who are useful to Him.

I enjoyed Brian's book so much, not only because we have been friends for years, but I have seen God working in his life. However, even if I didn't know him I would love the truth and realness of how he has come to know Jesus so personally through the things he has suffered, mistakes he has made and the wonderful love and mercy of our wonderful Lord.

Barbara Fairchild,
Country & Gospel Music Recording Artist
and most of all A Servant of God

If you've never heard Brian Arnold play the piano with one hand, you've missed one of life's most amazing musical experiences. So don't double your negative—don't miss reading this most inspiring and entertaining story of his life. You'll love every word of it!

Don Reid
The Statler Brothers

Brian Arnold knows about physical pain and emotional heartache. In *From Victim to Victory*, you will see how a broken boy struggled with issues that haunted him as he hobbled through his struggling teen years believing in God but not submitting to the Savior as Lord of his life. When we think we have it all figured out, like Brian, we don't—but God does. Through his own failures, he sends out a plea that others will not only turn to Jesus Christ, but will follow Him in every aspect of life.

Franklin Graham
President & CEO Billy Graham Evangelistic Association
Samaritan's Purse

TCT is committed to having one vision, one goal, one mission—touching the world with Jesus Christ. It's our passion! We do that by offering programs that feature people helping to share the Gospel in different ways. A new addition to our programming schedule is Brian Arnold, "America's Favorite One-Handed Pianist." Brian's show, "From Victim to Victory," is stirring and inspirational. His new book of the same title will bless your heart as you learn how he overcame life-shattering injuries and broken dreams to emerge into the light of God's glory. I heartily recommend *From Victim to Victory*.

Dr. Garth W. Coonce,
TCT President

America is still a God-fearing nation, and I know this because of the millions of visitors to our family-themed park, Silver Dollar City, SDC represents the best of our heritage and so do the people who make it come alive on a daily basis, Brian Arnold has been a key part of that family. His musical ability, which is considerable, is the backdrop for his amazing story of overcoming devastating injuries to emerge into a glorious victory. I recommend *From Victim to Victory* to you, without hesitation!

Jack Herschend

From Victim To Victory
A Story of Hope
by Brian Arnold
www.brianarnoldministries.com

First printing: November 2011
Second printing: October 2012

BRIAN ARNOLD MINISTRIES
40 Foust Lane
Hollow Rock, Tennessee 38342

www.brianarnoldministries.com
888-391-5247

Cover and Interior design by Brian Franklin, Well Done Productions, Mountain City, Tennessee and Brent Spurlock, Green Forest, Arkansas. Front cover photo by Kelsey Keeton, K Keeton Designs,
www.kkeetondesigns.com

Printed in the United States of America

Foreward

The revival had been on my schedule for a long time. When I began to do itinerant evangelism, I decided early on I would never ask about the size, location or denomination of the church asking me to come to preach. So when the call came from a small church in Rolla, Missouri, I gladly accepted the invitation. As the date for the revival drew near, I was informed that I would be ministering with a musician and singer named Brian Arnold. I'm certain that one thing Brian and I had in common is that we'd never heard of each other. But the pastor of the church was the confident that God would use us to bring revival to his congregation and city.

But there was a problem, actually several, on the day the revival services began. You see, I had been killed in a car crash several years earlier, Brian lost a leg and the use of his arm sometime before, and the pastor had lost his voice. Yes, a pastor who could not speak. The first night of the revival the pastor introduced Brian, himself and me as, "A cripple, a mute and a dead man."

Not exactly politically correct, but accurate nevertheless. Since that night, I have considered Brian a good friend. I've had the privilege of ministering with him several times. Now, you'll get to know Brian in his remarkable book *From Victim to Victory*. He is a man of many gifts, talents, and life-affirming experiences. Brian brings his warmth, self-effacing humor, and humility to every page. His book is biblically grounded and rich with illustrations and stories that give purpose and perspective. Brian Arnold's spiritual journey reflects his generation, warts and all. And yet he overcomes enough setbacks and tragedies to last several lifetimes. After a series of regrettable decisions and painful actions, Brian admits in this book, "I should have been honest from the start." In *From Victim to Victory*, he is!

You have to wonder after years of performing near the roller coasters of Silver Dollar City in Branson, Missouri, if Brian and those who love him would see the parallels to his rise and fall and rise again. Yes, the record shows, "it was his arm, too."

Today, Brian is a vibrant and extraordinarily gifted man with a humble heart. He didn't let his trials define him. He chose to let them refine him. And if I may be so bold, let me answer Brian's question, "What good is a one-handed piano player?"

A lot of good, Brother Brian! To your titles of singer, musician, composer, and preacher, you can now add ... author. May God bless you as you turn the pages of this book, the story of a very gifted man who did indeed turn a mess into a message.

Don Piper,

August, 2011

Contents

"The secret of a good sermon is to have a good beginning and a good ending, then having the two as close together as possible."

−George Burns

"Nothing splendid has ever been achieved except by those who dared believe that something inside them was superior to circumstance."

−Bruce Barton

"Long before He laid down earth's foundations, He had us in mind, had settled on us as the focus of His love, to be made whole and holy by His love."

Eph. 1:4 (The Message)

Introduction

"I am somebody!"

What an awesome thought. To believe that statement puts into perspective what happens to us in life. Those words can change how you feel or how you react to the curve balls thrown at you. And believe me, life knows how to throw curve balls! We try our dead-level best to dodge them but more times than not, they hit their targets and knock us flat on our backs.

I remember in my early teens, playing catch with Randall Lovelace. Randall and I spent countless hours practicing so that one day, we could play baseball for the St. Louis Cardinals.

I was never really any good at it but Randall was naturally gifted. He could throw a hard fastball that would practically knock me backwards. His specialty though, was the curve ball. *This pitch always scared me.* It appeared to be going in one direction and then at the last second it would go the opposite direction. If I didn't pay real close attention to the ball, I would end up with my glove in the wrong position and the ball would hit me upside the head, especially if one got away from him.

Needless to say, I experienced that one too many times. It was painful and I learned to dread having a curve ball thrown at me.

Just like in baseball, life throws us many curve balls. We learn to look for them and to fear them. When we're hit by them, many of us stand up and say, "I don't want to play this game anymore!"

We go home, throw our glove in the trash, get a bowl of ice cream —crawl up on the couch and decide to just become a spectator. God doesn't want you to give up and just be a spectator. Jesus said in John 10:10, "I have come that you might have life and to have it more abundantly!"

I am literally living proof that people can live abundant lives, no matter the junk thrown at them.

But how do we have abundant life while curve balls are constantly being thrown at us? For many of us, this sports analogy sequels into another: there are times when it seems the curve balls are coming at us from one of those practice machines, in which a whole series of balls streak toward us!

Where is that abundant life when you've been run over by a lawn mower and a semi-truck? How are you supposed to feel when you lose a child or you've just been told that you have cancer?

Curve balls come in all different speeds and variations. Some will hurt more than others. Some will hurt longer than others. One thing is for sure; pain is no respecter of persons.

In the following pages, I'll attempt to share some of my personal pain and struggles, but hopefully and more importantly, I hope you see how I've found the abundant life that Jesus promised. It starts with the recognition that *I am somebody*. You and I are not mere mistakes or coincidences, but we are "fearfully and wonderfully made." (Psalm 139:14 KJV)

God had us designed before He created the earth. Every single day is another opportunity to grow closer to becoming who God wants us to be, for us to realize who He created us to be. God will take every moment you give Him, to shape and to mold you into the person He designed before the earth was formed.

Think of it: in the epic dimension of forming the earth and the entire universe, God was thinking of you. Every person throughout history has mattered to God, and that's something we need to wrap our minds around. When you do this, you are able to see life "slow down."

It's like another sports analogy: football players who transition from one level to the next—high school to college, hopefully college to the pros—all talk about the point in practice or during a game in which things slow down for them. No longer is it chaotic and surreal; the game "slows down" and they get their bearings.

It's at that moment when they learn to really thrive in the game and let their natural abilities take over.

We are looking for that transition moment when life slows down enough for us to think that, yes, just maybe I'll survive!

It can happen for you, will happen for you if you turn it all over to the Source.

Are you willing to give Him this day, struggles and all? Or will you decide to feel sorry for yourself, throw your life in the trash, crawl up on the couch and become a spectator?

Look, I'm no martyr. I'm not a superman because of overcoming a whole series of cruel curve balls. I know something, though. I know something very special and rich, and defining:

You're special. God loves you. Jesus died on a cross for you. *"This is the day which the Lord hath made. We will rejoice and be glad in it!"* (Psalm 118:24 NKJV)

"It's a beautiful day made just for me

Your love fills me over and now I see

A little touch of Heaven here with You

Pushing the clouds back and breaking through

It's a beautiful day"

–Brian Arnold and Doug Beiden
(From the song "It's A Beautiful Day")

Brian at the Andy Williams Moon River Theater
in Branson, Missouri

"It is our attitude at the beginning of a difficult task, which more than anything else, will affect its successful outcome."

–William James

It is the Lord who goes before you. He will be with you; he will not fail you or forsake you. Do not fear or be dismayed.

Deuteronomy 31:8)

"I Need a Script Doctor!"

When one is able to move past focusing on the shag carpet, "John Denver" glasses, and conversations sprinkled with words like "groovy," it becomes clear that the feel-good themes of the classic television sitcom "The Brady Bunch" still resonate with viewers—forty years on!

I grew up watching this show, like millions of Americans. Each week, a semi-crisis was dealt with by level-headed parents, assorted neighbors, and, of course, the wit and wisdom of Alice, the ultimate maid! Whether it was Jan's term paper, or Greg's faltering romances, the Brady's always managed to survive and thrive.

This entire fictional family was the brainchild of the masterful Hollywood producer, Sherwood Schwartz.

The New Jersey-born Schwartz (aged 94 at the time of this writing, and still going strong!) began his career writing jokes for Bob Hope's radio show in the 40's, moving to "The Adventures of Ozzie and Harriet," and eventually reached the pantheon of producing with such iconic programs as "Gilligan's Island," and earlier, served as script supervisor for "My Favorite Martian." He even wrote the theme songs for "Gilligan's Island" and "The Brady Bunch." Truly a renaissance man!

As a kid, I watched his shows and they never failed to make me feel good. All was right in those worlds.

There was just one problem: idyllic settings that go on without end are fictional. They don't really exist, except on back movie lots, and in the imaginations of gifted storytellers.

The time would come in my life—as it does in everyone's life— when the fantasy existence of the Bradys and Gilligan couldn't help me. I encountered difficulties that challenged every energy reserve I'd ever have.

In fact, in middle age now, as I reflect on some of the things that have happened to me, I identify more with the book by Danny Sugerman and Jerry Hopkins, *No One Here Gets Out Alive*, chronicling the tragic comet known as Jim Morrison.

There was no Sherwood Schwartz to write the script of my life!

I've always been a person who rolls with the punches, as they say—to the best of my ability. Sure, I've had some setbacks to deal with, and believe me, I haven't always been an angel in the way I've handled those setbacks. As you journey through this story with me, you'll discover just what those setbacks have been and just how important, literally, it has been to me to stand on my own two feet.

You'll discover, though, that during my travels through the odyssey of my life, I wasn't always intent on overcoming trials.

At least, not in the beginning.

By 1994, I had overcome some things and had developed into a fairly successful musician. I'd been blessed to have worked with quite a few multi-talented singers, songwriters, and musicians, and had arrived at a place where I was working a very nice gig at the now-fabled Silver Dollar City, in Branson, Missouri. I had become a full-fledged member of a gospel quartet!

This was a true dream come true. I'd grown up privileged to hear the sounds of legendary quartets like the Blackwood Brothers, ranging from the iconic-but-tragic R.W. Blackwood, to long-touring James Blackwood.

In any event, by early 1994 I was poised to have a nice career as a gospel singer, and it was my wonderful fortune to link-up with some incredible talents. Chosen Few, a gospel quartet that I had the privilege of helping get started, was about to embark on a winter tour at the beginning of their second full-time year of existence.

One thing you have to understand about our "neck of the woods" is that winters, while not on the scale of Minnesota's gargantuan snowdrifts, still pack a wallop in terms of ice. In fact, we always count on at least a week of being "ice-bound" as we see the clear "slippery stuff" coating our mountain roads.

Still, as I peeked out the window on that January morning, I eagerly anticipated our upcoming concert in Marshfield, Missouri. Honestly, there was no doubt we were embarking on a significant tour that would lead to bigger and bigger things.

I finished packing the last of my things and headed out into the chilly morning. Pulling out of the driveway to meet up with my quartet mates, I breathed a heart-felt thanks.

The overcast skies and cautious line of drivers on I-44 caused me to say *brrrrrrrr* to no one in particular. It would be nice to set up in a warm, inviting church!

To this day, I remember that I was doing 57 mph; I don't know why. It is just locked into my memory bank.

Perhaps my mind was so concentrated, I was focusing on relatively unimportant details.

Maybe that's why I never saw the semi-truck, until it was too late.

Ice. Snow. Wreckage littering the highway.

It all seemed a perfect metaphor for my life.

I was still conscious after the collision, and I'm not sure that was a good thing. My broken body was cold that January day, as my friends raced to free me from the mangled vehicle. In those moments, I had time to think...

It's true what they say—in a life-and-death-moment, you jet through the wormhole of your life to that point, re-living events at break-neck speed...

"Our lives are not determined by what happens to us but by how we react to what happens, not by what life brings to us, but by the attitude we bring to life. A positive attitude causes a chain reaction of positive thoughts, events, and outcomes. It is a catalyst; a spark that creates extraordinary results."

- Anonymous

"In everything give thanks."

1 Thess. 5:18 (KJV)

Chapter 2

Without A Leg
To Stand On

In the summer of 1973, my life would forever change. Our family lived in Maryville, a bucolic town tucked into the northwest corner of Missouri. It had been the home of, among others, Dale Carnegie, and one George S.E. Vaughn, a Confederate spy whose pardon had been the last official act of President Lincoln, moments before he left for Ford's Theatre.

During that fateful summer, more than once, I felt that I was hanging by a thread, and was in desperate need of a pardon for the trial I was facing.

My parents, Bob and Shirley Arnold, had moved to the area several years earlier to attend college at Northwest Missouri State University. My father's parents, Glendon and Oma Arnold, had also moved to Maryville. We were transplants from Southeast Missouri. The rest of our family and relatives lived nowhere close to us.

I always looked forward to summertime because that usually meant a trip down south to visit Mom's parents, Grover and Gladys Horn. They lived on a small milk farm outside West Plains, Missouri. For a six-year-old boy who lived in the "city," this was like going to Disneyland.

Those days were idyllic!

At Grandma's farm, there was an adventure waiting around every corner—cows, chickens and pigs. A big barn where the cows got milked—it also had a hayloft, a real hayloft!

I also learned that cows take baths, too...in the backyard pond. There were three big gardens filled with corn, green beans, cucumbers, and tomatoes. Grandpa had not one, but three tractors that he had taken me for rides.

Oh, I loved it so. Often, I think back to those days and wish every child could experience it...miles away from pain and suffering and anxiety.

My Uncle Gene, who lived on the farm with my grandparents, would let me tag along with him to do chores. Even though I really wasn't much help, he would pay me in silver dollars, anyway. At the end of each day, he'd press a shiny dollar into my hand, and as they say, Lord, I thought I was rich.

And Catfish Hunter and Tug McGraw had nothing on me. When I wasn't throwing fastballs with walnuts at the propane tank in the backyard, or helping milk the cows, I was hiding away down in the basement of Grandma's house exploring every piece of old furniture. I just knew that buried somewhere in their house was a treasure waiting for me to find it!

Perhaps it was the Missouri in me, or me in it, that reminded me from time to time of those lads who skittered and skipped through Mark Twain's imagination. I half-expected to see Tom Sawyer and Huck Finn come 'round the corner of the barn.

The expectation for my summer visit to West Plains in 1973 was no different from past visits. How was I to know that my life was going to change so drastically?

I'm not even sure that I was aware of the fact that we were moving that fall to Albany, Missouri, so that Dad could take a basketball coaching position at the high school there, or that Grandma Arnold was moving back to Thayer, Missouri. Grandpa had died the year before, and the place just wasn't the same without him.

No sir, at the age of six, all you can think about is going on an adventure. And that adventure was a Memorial Day weekend trip to West Plains, where Grandma's milk cows were waiting for me.

I suppose it was a summer day like most: the sun shining bright, and not a cloud in the sky. However, the day had started long before the sun had come up. I slept in the room where my Uncle Gene slept and it was he that woke me up that early summer morning to go milk the cows. I know to him this was a twice-daily chore, but to a six-year-old boy who lived in the "city" of Maryville, this was like waking up early on Christmas morning.

I was practically awake anyway.

The bed I slept in was right by an open window. (Can there be a better sample of heaven anywhere than an open window bringing in a cool night breeze down on the farm?).

I quickly looked out to find that we had successfully gotten up before the sun. It was like nighttime; yet it wasn't...it was *milking time*! I quickly got dressed and followed my uncle out of the house and down the lane to the barn where my grandparents already were. They were always the first to get to the barn.

As I walked into the barn, I saw a light bulb hanging from the ceiling, barely lighting up the room and I could hear my grandpa out back of the barn calling in the cows.

Grandma had an old AM radio that she always turned on first thing and I can still remember Bobby Helm's voice on KWPM ("Keep West Plains Moving") that welcomed the sun's emergence every morning. Usually it was the news and weather on first, followed by the farm report and then country music would serenade us as we went about milking the cows. Many a time Merle Haggard would sing us back home to the sound of our own unique tune, as the spray of fresh milk hit the buckets with a rhythm all its own.

Grandma had names for all her milk cows, although to be honest, I don't remember any of them now. I just remember that I was allowed to pet them while they were eating their feed and being milked, but I was always warned not to get too close to their hind legs because you never knew when one of them might kick you!

Looking back at it now, it all seems so simple, yet it was thrilling to me. I didn't have an iPod, video games or things like that when I was a kid. I did however, have an imagination and it was like being in the Old West in Grandma's barn. I was the Lone Ranger and

Uncle Gene was Tonto, and we fought off the bandits from stealing Grandma's cows. Boy, the fire of an imagination!

After the West was won, it was time for breakfast. This is when my parents would get up and join the day. I can still smell the homemade bread that Grandma made and she didn't even have a bread maker! I loved to eat cereal at Grandma's house because instead of milk with my cereal, I used real cream. Heaven!

After breakfast, it was on to more adventures. At some point that morning, my dad decided to help my grandparents by mowing their yard for them. Grandpa had a John Deere riding lawn mower with an actual steering wheel. Back then, most mowers only had handlebars like a bicycle.

My younger sister, Shelley, and I were excited that Dad was going to mow the yard because this meant that we would get to take turns riding in his lap on the mower and using the steering wheel to drive. (My youngest sister, Amy, was not yet born.)

Of course, in my rich imagination, I was driving out on the open highway and my sister was the hitchhiker I would pull over to lend a hand to...and then she would steal my car!

It's almost funny now—but not in a comical way—how all that Opie Taylor existence ended so suddenly for me.

What happened next, no one should have to go through. I was waiting to use my superpowers to overtake the evil hitchhiker, who stole my car, to drive by again (I was waiting for *my* turn to ride), when I heard Mom holler and motioned me to come to her.

I reluctantly headed towards her, fearful that I might miss my chance to stop the evildoer (I didn't want to miss my turn). She wanted me to inform Dad and Shelley that it was time to take a break from mowing and come inside to eat. I turned around and headed back towards them to deliver the message.

Dad and Shelley were mowing around the big bush in Grandma's front yard and I came along the left side of them yelling to get their attention. Dad veered left with the mower to miss the bush and I went left too but the grass was still moist from the morning dew. I slipped and the mower drove right over the top of my left leg and part of my right foot.

Dad says that he still remembers the "thud" of the blade cutting through the bone of my left leg, killing the mower's engine instantly. Those few seconds are still surreal to all of us. I was so stunned, the pain didn't reach my consciousness immediately.

Mom began running from the house towards us as Dad sat Shelley down on the ground and quickly threw the mower off of me. He then yelled to my mother to pick me up as he headed to get the car.

It all happened so fast. *No time to even think.* As we headed towards West Plains Memorial Hospital in our Chevy Impala—Dad drove over a hundred miles per hour—my mother held me in one arm and in the other arm she held my left leg, held on only by the Achilles tendon. It was a ghastly scene.

Besides the gruesome wound and the emotional trauma they both felt, my parents had to keep their wits about them. This they did; both were magnificent in caring for me.

Without crying out or shedding a single tear, I looked up at my mother and asked very calmly, "Will I be back in time to help milk the cows this evening?" It was the innocent question of a boy who had not endured tragedy, until now.

Little did I know that I would never be back to life, as I had known it. *Back to life.* It would be years before I understood the full impact of what that day would mean to my life, or to the lives of my family.

Dad must have found it nearly impossible that day to hope that something good could come from all this, let alone in all things to give thanks. How do you find peace when your only son has been mangled in a lawn-mowing accident?

Where do you find the good in life when you get to the hospital and the doctors tell you that they are more concerned about your son living than whether or not they can re-attach his leg?

The human experience tells us that we all arrive at a place where we ask the deep questions of life. How do you find the good in life?

I can tell you that it comes from a daily, personal relationship with Jesus. If you choose to rely on God only when you're in trouble, faith will be hard to find. Faith takes practice. According to Romans 10:17, "Faith comes by hearing and hearing by the Word of God." The word is *hearing,* which is present-tense. It's a current action, not something you've done in the past.

Hebrews 11:1 says, "Faith is the *substance* of things hoped for, the *evidence* of things not seen." When you can't see how things are ever going to get any better, faith sees you through. I can tell you through the experience you are reading about, that faith and genuine peace come from years lived—relying on God when you literally have nowhere else to turn.

Faith is a lifestyle, not a quick fix to your problem!

Don't wait until your son has been mauled by a lawn mower to decide that you need faith in God. Start now. Develop your own personal relationship with Jesus today.

Your circumstance, dear reader, is different from mine. But the Source of life, whom I've just described, will "customize" a plan just for your needs.

"I count it all joy to serve the King

He has redeemed me, that's why I can sing

Depending on Him, I need nothing more

Though sometimes I suffer, I count it all joy"

–Brian Arnold and Chresten Tomlin
(From the song "I Count It All Joy")

Brian with his daughter
Kelsey Rae Keeton

Brian with his wife Diane,
and daughter, Kelsey

Brian's daughter, Kerrigan

"There are people who are always anticipating trouble, and in this way they manage to enjoy many sorrows that never really happen to them."

–Josh Billings

"For to be carnally minded is death: but to be spiritually minded is life and peace"

Romans 8:6 (KJV)

Chapter 3

Being Different

Eventually, I would find myself on a two-hour ambulance ride to Springfield, Missouri because the hospital in West Plains was not equipped to deal with injuries like mine, and they didn't have helicopters for hospitals back then. This was the longest ride of Dad's life.

He became very frustrated because the ambulance driver wouldn't drive fast enough. The driver also didn't turn his sirens on. Mom thinks today that the reason he didn't have them on was so that I wouldn't become too upset with all the noise. Whatever the reason, we couldn't get to Cox Hospital in Springfield fast enough to suit my dad.

Once we finally arrived, the gravity of my situation began to set in. My doctor was a man by the name of Bruce Shackter. He was a very calm and gentle man. Dr. Shackter proceeded to tell my parents that the first priority was not my leg, but my life. I had lost so much blood, that when I arrived at the hospital in Springfield, I literally had no pulse.

For my part, the experience was much like you'd expect from a TV show: a fast-motion collage of lights, people yelling, and prep work. I do believe my poor parents had it worse than I did in those first minutes and hours.

A Horrible Dream—A Father Remembers

The day that Brian lost his leg was the most horrific day of my life. I remember I kept saying to myself as we were speeding to the hospital in West Plains, Let this be a dream.

Sadly, it was not a dream but a reality. I remember thinking what have I done, since I was the one driving the lawn mower, I changed the boy's life forever. I can still hear the thumping of the leg as it was under the mower.

My father, Glendon, came to mind as we traveled to Springfield in the ambulance. He had polio at the age of two and was left with a severely deformed left leg with no muscle strength. So, I knew the difficulties he had with every day life, and I knew Brian would be facing the same kinds of obstacles. He did not have an easy childhood but he accepted it with courage and determination.

–Bob Arnold

Mom says that she had never once thought about the possibility that I could lose my life. All she had been concerned about was getting my leg reattached. Now my parents were faced with the realization that I might not live. Isn't it alarming how life can change so quickly? One moment, we were enjoying a day in the country, the next my life hung in the balance.

This was a very difficult time for my family because not only were we a long way from our home in Maryville, but we were now two hours away from my grandparents' home in West Plains. My parents were forced to alternate staying with my aunt and her husband in Nixa, Missouri while I was in the hospital, but one of them remained there with me the entire time.

The next hours and days were a blur for me. Thankfully, the wonderful care and skill of the doctors and staff saved my life. I well remember though realizing that my leg was gone. It is a bizarre feeling knowing that part of your body is no longer there. In the intervening years, I have developed a real empathy for our troops in harm's way, as well. At least in that sense, I can relate.

I would eventually recover, but I lost my left leg below the knee and all the toes on my right foot were paralyzed except the big toe. It seems it has been my lot in life to have partial usage of several appendages! (We'll get to that.)

After my recovery, we returned home to Maryville, but only for a short time. One memory that will always stay with me is the handmade toy box—full of toys—that the city of Maryville gave me upon my return home. I had Christmas for a month!

We soon moved from Maryville to Albany, Missouri—not far away, and still a baseball throw from Iowa. As with several places we lived, I had the benefit of living in an idyllic, "Mayberry type" community. The red-brick Gentry County Courthouse, with its tall spire, was a sight I loved to sit and look at. I did that a lot...to sit and think.

To say that growing up with an artificial leg was difficult would be an understatement. Moving to a new town is difficult enough all on its own, but being the new kid with a "wooden" leg could be downright miserable.

I learned very quickly to disguise it as much as possible. That proved to be a challenge, though, because my new leg had rough edges around the knee. I was constantly wearing holes in my pant's leg and then it would protrude through, reminding everyone that I was indeed different. Then as if that wasn't bad enough, the wool stump socks I was forced to wear on my leg would begin to smell by the end of a school day because of the perspiration. Talk about feeling like I didn't fit in...

Losing a leg at a young age also means a lot of growth spurts, which means a lot of leg adjustments resulting in sores and scabs. That meant that I needed to use crutches in order to give my leg some needed rest. I *hated* using crutches. I think as a child, crutches are only fun for the first couple of days, then the realization that you can't run and play with the other kids sets in. This created isolation from kids who already thought I was different.

Lately, there's been a lot of talk in the news of bullying in schools; it seems that school administrators are determined to do something about it. Not in my day! If you were the target of a bully, it meant you went to the school of hard knocks—literally.

I can vividly remember one boy who tormented me almost every day at school. He constantly made fun of me and referred to me as "Wooden Leg." This is a bit different from being called "Four Eyes" for wearing glasses.

Although now that I'm older and I know he didn't represent how all the kids felt, I allowed his comments to affect me more than they should have. I focused on his words and began to feel like I was less important than everyone else. This was the beginning of the inferiority complex that would shape my whole life. My identity in a very real sense was chained to that artificial leg.

To compound problems, my dad was now the high school basketball coach. Dad had been somewhat of a high school sports standout when he was younger. I was naturally very drawn to sports because of Dad's involvement with it. I still recall going to his basketball practices and running around the gym while the team did drills or practiced free throws.

He would occasionally let me take bus trips with him and his team to away games and I'd sit on the bench watching and dreaming of playing in the "big game." The "big game" however never came. Nobody wants a boy with a "wooden" leg on the basketball team. I also found the same to be true with teams for dodgeball, softball, baseball or anything that required running. All of this continued to reinforce that I was different and it was all because of my "wooden" leg.

Why couldn't I be like Col. Steve Austin, the "Six Million Dollar Man"? Steve Austin was my hero in 1974. My hero was actually an actor by the name of Lee Majors who played Steve Austin on my favorite TV show. Here was a guy who had been in a terrible plane crash, lost both of his legs, an arm and an eye and they said, "We can rebuild him. We can make him better than he was. Better. Stronger. Faster." Steve could outrun anybody, see farther than anybody, bend steel with his arm and be cool all at the same time. Why couldn't they fix me to be like Steve?

For Christmas in 1974, my parents got me the Six Million Dollar Man doll with the space rocket that turned into an operating table. Wow! I loved it...yes, I loved playing with this doll. I'm man enough to admit it! I also had Batman and Robin, Aqua Man, Superman and Big Jim and Big Jeff, who came with an RV camper and boat. Talk about losing yourself in adventures and international intrigue.

So there...go ahead and laugh; I played with dolls.

The same Christmas I got my Six Million Dollar Man doll, I also got a new Statler Brothers record entitled, "Country Music: Then and Now." The Statlers: Don and Harold Reid, Phil Balsley, Jimmy Fortune (and the late, great tenor he replaced, Lew DeWitt)—I get the impression, were a bit like me as kids. Our imaginations sometimes ran wild.

The new record was when the world of "Roadhog" was opened up to me. If you've never heard the Statler Brothers do their Saturday Morning Radio Show with Lester Moran—the old Roadhog and his Cadillac Cowboys—then you need to add this to your collection. I'll just say that Dad and I had a great laugh that Christmas and many laughs since over "Roadhog." *"Aw Right!"*

So now, here I am in a new town with a new leg, with a dad who's a new *basketball coach* and dealing with feelings of being inferior and different when Mom gets a "new" idea.

Although my parents have never fully realized how inferior I felt growing up, my mom did realize that I needed something to do to fill in the gap of not playing sports. That "new" idea was a piano she saw advertised in the newspaper in the classified section.

She called on the ad to find that the lady was actually giving the piano away. The only problem was that it was located a couple of hours away and some other people were on their way to look at it. My mom, being the shrewd negotiator that she is, told the woman she would give her twenty-five dollars for the piano sight unseen if she would hold it for her. This woman quickly realized that twenty-five dollars was better than zero dollars and accepted my mother's offer.

This is where one of those weird twists of life entered my own shattered life.

We were now the proud owners of a Schiller upright piano and I was now forced to take piano lessons. The lessons weren't so bad I guess; it was just the practicing that I loathed. I was required to practice thirty minutes every day, first thing when getting home from school. We were not a musical family by any means, so I had zero interest in playing the piano, especially when the songs I had to learn made no sense to me. For a Steve Austin wannabe, this was torture!

Now, the piano was located in the basement where I would occasionally find myself unsupervised during practice time. This would be great as long as Mom wasn't paying close attention, because if I made just enough noise on the piano she would think I was doing my lesson.

One day though, this backfired on me. I was sitting in the basement alone putting in my time, when I decided that I could play my lesson on the piano with my nose; probably my own version of the "Jimi Hendrix Experience."

This was a tactical error on my part, though. Playing one note at a time with my nose would cause my mother to become suspicious of the song I was "playing" and she decided to sneak down the stairs. She was not amused and therefore my practice time became more supervised.

I *did* enjoy music though, and just not the selections I was being forced to learn. Dad had a den in the basement of our Albany house where he and I would listen to his reel-to-reel player for what seemed to me to be hours at a time. I still have that Wollensak reel-to-reel player today. Little did Dad know that he was planting seeds into my life that would later forever shape the person I would become.

We loved to listen to the music of the Statler Brothers. He had two of their records on reel-to-reel, "Bed Of Roses" and "Pictures Of Moments To Remember." That music would truly become a part of me. Even to this day, I know the words to each and every song on both of those records and if I hear one of those songs, I'm instantly transported back to that den in the basement of our Albany home. What my dad didn't know was that inside of me a spark went off and a love for quartet music was started. Not even I would fully realize the impact the Statler Brothers' music had on my life until years later. The way they have been able to tell stories down through the years, using their voices as instruments...well, as I said, it has been a sweet inspiration.

As I look back now, I can plainly see the bad seeds that the enemy was planting in my life and the good seeds that God was planting in my life. At the time I was too close to it to clearly see this simultaneous activity, and probably way too young to even recognize it.

Today, though, I'm filled with the confidence that God is always putting things into my life to bless me. His blessings are not always immediate, though. It's easy to think that the devil is winning because his schemes almost always have an immediate negative effect.

More often than not, we focus on the bad seeds that have been planted in our lives. I know I sure did. All I could wrap my mind around was what I didn't have. "Oh, woe is me!"

In Psalm 1:3 God says, "Blessed is the man who is like a tree **planted** by the rivers of water, that brings forth His fruit in His season..." No matter what the devil may try to plant into your life, if you are a child of God, you are blessed! God has already planted the seeds of blessing into your life.

You have been planted by the rivers of water. And that water is Jesus. God *will* bring forth His fruit (His blessings) in your life, in His season (when it's best for you). The question is, which seeds are you watering? What are you focusing on? Trust God right now that He's working in your life to bring about those blessings that He may have planted in you years ago.

"If you're the least bit different

Then there's something wrong with you

And the world tries its best to pull you down...

But I will carry on this way until Jesus comes"

–Brian Arnold and Niles Borop
(From the song "I Will Carry On This Way")

Brian with youth specialist,
Steven Sexton

Brian with pastor friend,
Dennis Hustead

Brian with TCT Host, Julie Nolan

Brian's daughter, Kerrigan

"The world is not respectable; it is mortal, tormented, confused, deluded forever; but it is shot through with beauty, with love, with glints of courage and laughter; and in these, the spirit blooms timidly, and struggles to the light amid the thorns."

–George Santayana

Fierce troubles came down on the people of those churches, pushing them to the very limit. The trial exposed their true colors: They were incredibly happy, though desperately poor.

2 Corinthians 8:2 (The Message)

The Move To West Plains

In the summer of 1976, my family left northern Missouri to move back to West Plains. It was definitely a homecoming for Mom because she had been born and raised in West Plains. Suddenly, we found ourselves living around family and that was a good feeling.

Now, instead of being hours away from Grandma and Grandpa Horn's, we were minutes away, plus Grandma Arnold was only thirty minutes down the road in Thayer. West Plains was known for being the hometown of country music legends Porter Wagoner and Jan Howard. Dick Van Dyke was actually born there too, but since his parents were just traveling through, he doesn't claim it as anything.

The move to West Plains was exciting to me for a number of reasons, but none more exciting than getting to pick the color of my new room, green—my favorite color. Mom and Dad were buying a brand-new house, and even though it was quite a bit smaller than the Albany house, it was exciting just the same.

Unlike our previous home, this one had a big yard, almost three acres. It was an adventure waiting to happen. What I didn't realize at the time was that those three acres of adventurous fun would become three acres of lawn mowing. Now before you think it, my parents were not callous and inconsiderate for assigning me the job of mowing the yard. Just because I had lost a leg under a lawn mower didn't mean that I had to live my life in fear and dread of them. This was but one example of my parents' wisdom in helping me cope with the accident.

To this day it doesn't bother me in the least to be around a lawn mower, but I can say that as a kid growing up, three acres was a lot to mow and I dreaded that for sure.

Living in West Plains also meant that I could help my Uncle Gene more regularly, which meant more silver dollars for me. I wish I still had all those silver dollars that he paid me!

I think Uncle Gene just liked having me around. He was a very strong and large man. I don't mean that he was overweight, but that he was a big man. He spent all his life working on that farm until his health demanded that he go into a nursing home. Uncle Gene was a man of few words, I think mostly because of a speech impediment. When he did speak it was fast and slurred and some may have considered him to be different, but in my eyes he was a hero.

I always felt that he and I shared a sort of bond because of my leg and his speech impediment. I know for sure that we enjoyed each other's company.

We cut, raked and baled hay, and he taught me how to drive a tractor all by myself. We built pigpens, put up fences, and he taught me how to drive a nail with a hammer and to keep a watchful for eye out for the electric fence.

We cut firewood and fixed tractors. He showed me how to handle an ax and taught me the importance of "Goop" (this was used to get grease off of your hands). We fed the cows hay and the chickens got corn. And every Saturday morning, Uncle Gene and I, along with Grandma, would go down to our church, Bethel Baptist Church, and clean it from top to bottom.

Bethel Baptist Church is a little country church on a dirt road outside of West Plains; my family attended regularly every Sunday morning. It's where my Grandma Horn and Uncle Gene had attended most of their lives.

My uncle always sat on the very front row on the right for every service and he never once forgot his Bible. The pastor's name was Reverend Greeney. I'm sure he had a first name but I only knew him as Reverend Greeney. My recollection of this preacher was that he was old and boring. I'm sure the truth was that I was young and inattentive!

(When I recall these days—I think I've already established that I had a wonderful childhood in most respects—it's almost as if I'm replaying a black-and-white movie like "To Kill a Mockingbird." I learned a lot about life growing up in small towns filled with good, solid people.)

Every Saturday morning was church cleaning day. Grandma would start dusting upstairs in the sanctuary. Uncle Gene and I would start in the basement. My job was to empty the trashcans and sweep the concrete floors. This was not an easy or quick job because there were so many metal-folding chairs that had to be moved before I could sweep.

Uncle Gene paid me eight silver dollars every Saturday. That was good money for doing the Lord's work! Although the work was boring, I did manage to find a way to help pass the time. In one of the Sunday school classrooms there was an old record player with one record. That record was "The Great Gospel Quartets of 1965."

I played this record every Saturday morning and soaked in the incredible music of these quartets. The first song on the record was by the Blackwood Brothers and it was called "O What A Savior." I was enthralled by this music.

The Stamps, the Statesmen, the Prophets, the Rebels, the Blue Ridge Quartet, and the list goes on and on. I learned to sing every song by heart. From "Sing Your Blues Away" to "It's Different Now," to the original Oak Ridge Boys singing, "He Will Never Let Me Down." Yes, there was actually an incarnation of the Oaks before Joe Bonsall raced up and down the stage!

What great melodies and intricate harmonies! I fell in love with the harmony of the Statler Brothers, but I also fell in love with Gospel music through that old record I found in the basement of Bethel Baptist Church. No one ever claimed to own that record and I was eventually told that I could have it. I still have it in my record collection today and I have personally recorded many of those songs I first heard while cleaning the church with my Uncle Gene.

Recently, I watched one of the Bill Gaither specials on television, with Gospel greats like Vestal Goodman, Squire Parsons, and J.D.

Sumner singing the old favorites. What a wonderful time, and what a wonderful, real faith those singers had. They sang for the Lord.

My uncle contracted thyroid cancer several years later and while having surgery to remove his thyroid, one of his vocal chords was paralyzed, forcing him to have a permanent tracheotomy. This once strong and mighty man began to wither away and eventually ended up with Parkinson's disease. He finally became too much for my grandma to take care of and went to live in a nursing home.

He passed away several years later, but he never let a day of his life go by that he didn't read his Bible and pray. Uncle Gene will always remain a strong and mighty man in my eyes, and I owe him so much for all that he taught me. He never once looked at me as a cripple. He was my friend and I loved him very much.

One of the more important aspects of our move to West Plains was the change in my dad's vocation. Dad had grown tired of coaching and on the advice of a friend had gone back to college to get his degree in school administration. What this meant for me was that my dad was now the principal of my new school, Glenwood Elementary.

Glenwood was a Kindergarten-through-8th-grade school outside West Plains and I was now officially a Glenwood Mustang. Being the new kid at school is tough enough, but add to the mix an inferiority complex, a "wooden" leg and "Oh by the way, my dad is the new principal!" and you have a recipe for isolation. Dad was now Mr. Arnold to me during the day. To say that he was strict would probably not be doing him justice. Dad very seldom smiled while he was at school.

I was now entering the fourth grade and my teacher was Mr. Bridges. This was the first time I had ever had a male teacher and this guy was cool! He really made fourth grade a lot of fun. I can especially remember math races. This was a game by which two kids stood on a line halfway back in the room away from the chalkboard and waited to hear the math problem, then the word "Go!"

They would then run to the chalkboard, write out the math problem and try to be the first to solve it. Even though this game involved running, I enjoyed it all the same and was actually pretty good at it. This was also the same year of the presidential election between Gerald Ford and Jimmy Carter. The only reason I remember that is because Mr. Bridges held a mock election in our classroom and I was the deciding vote. I'll let you guess whom I voted for.

Fourth grade was also memorable because I was saved in the fall of 1976 in a revival at Bethel Baptist Church. This was back when revival meetings were held for two weeks at a time. Today, you're lucky if a revival lasts for three days. I got saved on the last meeting of the revival. I often wonder how many people today would be saved if we weren't so inconvenienced by a revival lasting too long.

I don't remember the name of the evangelist, but I do remember how I felt. The Spirit of God was all over me that week. I knew something was wrong but I wasn't sure what I needed to do about it. I remember sitting in the back row on an old wooden bench that creaked with the slightest movement. Mom and Dad always knew if I was getting out of hand by the creaking of the bench.

I can honestly say that it wasn't so much the words that the evangelist spoke, but it was the Spirit drawing me. The invitation time during that revival seemed to last forever. I would stand there with my hands gripping that pew and being overwhelmed with the feeling that I needed to walk that aisle and grab his hand like he was asking me.

Several of my friends were getting saved throughout that week, but I wasn't real sure what to do. I remember coming home Saturday night after the revival meeting and lying in my bed thinking, "This guy will be gone after tomorrow and I don't feel any of this when Reverend Greeney preaches." I now understand that it wasn't the messenger but the message that was penetrating my heart, but at the time I didn't know what to think.

I remember calling Mom into my bedroom and telling her about what I was feeling. She explained to me that I needed to be saved and that God was convicting me of my sins during those invitation times. She explained that Jesus had died on a cross for my sins and that I needed to give my heart to him in order for me to go to heaven. She then encouraged me to think about all of this and then to follow the tugging on my heart.

The next morning I sat on the front row with Uncle Gene; that way I didn't have far to walk come invitation time. I couldn't tell you what the sermon was about that day, but I can tell you that when the invitation time came I felt the Spirit of God come over me, drawing on me and that evangelist stood at the altar and said, "Today is the day of salvation. Who here today wants to be saved?"

I left that front pew and stepped toward him. Taking his hand I said, "I want to be saved." We knelt down at the altar and he opened up his Bible and showed me that I was a sinner, but that God had loved me so much that He had sent His only Son, Jesus, to die on a cross for me. He showed me Romans 10:9 that says, "That if you confess with your mouth, 'Jesus is Lord,' and believe in your heart that God raised Him from the dead, you will be saved." (NIV)

That Sunday morning, right there at the altar in the Bethel Baptist Church, I gave my heart and life to Jesus. I was baptized that same afternoon in Crawford's Creek. I know that baptism is very special and it has a lot of meaning to me, but I remember that day as being the first time I ever got in water with my artificial leg on. The next day at school, Mr. Bridges asked the class if anyone did anything exciting over the weekend. I quickly raised my hand and proudly informed the whole fourth grade that I had been saved, and I've been saved ever since then.

I had friends at Glenwood but I never really felt like I fitted in. I was the odd man out. We had some great basketball teams while I attended Glenwood and I was on the floor for every game...I was the "manager" who occasionally got to sit by Coach Taylor. I kept the stats, got the guys water and towels, but I never once got to play in the "big" game.

My eighth grade year while everyone was getting awards for their achievements, I was awarded the spirit award. It was a nice award and I appreciated it, but it wasn't the same as the others.

There were times throughout my years at Glenwood that I really resented being the principal's kid. I once received a spanking from my dad in front of a teacher because she demanded that I not get special treatment. The sad part was that I hadn't done what I was being accused of. Dad later apologized to me when we were at home, saying he had believed me but felt he would be looked at as giving his son a break.

Feeling like an outcast is no fun and you usually attract other outcasts. My best friend while attending Glenwood was Sheldon Turner, another misfit and outcast. Sheldon was the guy who had done and seen it all.

He was the product of a broken home and a boy who could spin a tale faster than you could blink. I believe he acquired this skill as a coping mechanism.

He and I became fast friends. We spent countless hours together doing all sorts of things. Sheldon taught me how to fish. He told me about his secret fishing hole and he *guaranteed* I could catch as many fish as I wanted.

Of course, I told him that I didn't believe him, so he took me to it one day and sure enough, I never caught so many fish in my life. I never knew until much later that the place he had taken me to fish was a restricted stock pond. No wonder we caught so many fish! It's a wonder that we didn't get caught.

Sheldon also taught me how to ride a motorcycle. I always thought that he looked so cool riding his motorcycle and I desperately wanted to be cool so I asked him to teach me. The problem with this idea was that Dad had strictly forbidden me to be on the motorcycle, let alone ride it myself. But after numerous pleas, I finally convinced him to let me ride it with the promise that I wouldn't get it out of first gear.

Anyone that knows anything about riding motorcycles knows that it is impossible to ride one without getting it out of first gear. Dad however, was not one of those people. By the time he came to pick me up from Sheldon's that day I was flying down that dirt road, an accomplished motorcycle rider. Dad was not amused, but he said nothing other than, "Looks to me like you were going faster than first gear." I just smiled.

Sheldon was another person that accepted me as being normal. Although as we grew older, we grew apart, I never will forget the adventures we shared while fishing, hunting or riding motorcycles.

Around 1978, Dad became a Gideon. This is a ministry that provides Bibles to hotels, foreign countries and back then even fifth-grade classes. I'll never forget receiving a little New Testament when the Gideons came to visit our class. You won't see that happening in today's world. Dad would go to churches and speak on the need for more Bibles in the world and try to get people to sponsor the ministry of the Gideons.

Then in 1980, Dad surrendered to the ministry to preach. He began filling in for different preachers for various reasons, which meant occasionally we would miss going to church with Grandma and Uncle Gene to go hear Dad preach at other churches. Although I was proud of my dad, it now meant that he was my father, my principal and my pastor. That is a lethal combination for any kid, but especially for one with an inferiority complex and a "wooden" leg.

I suppose that the single most important thing that happened to me after moving to West Plains, outside of being saved, was the decision I made to start piano lessons again. When we first got to West Plains I was so elated not to have to take piano lessons. I didn't have a piano teacher and I had convinced Mom not to bother with finding one.

Besides, I never got to play songs that I actually knew anyway. It was always the rudimentary pieces designed more for technique and that was incredibly boring to me. Yet, there was a boy at school named Jeff Duncan who played piano. The thing that caught my attention was that he was playing songs that the other kids knew, and he was a very popular kid.

This got me to thinking. I wanted to play songs I could sing. I loved music, I just didn't like the songs I'd been forced to learn. So, one day I decided I wanted to learn one of my favorite Statler Brothers songs, "Susan When She Tried."

Now, Dad had a Toyota Corolla with an 8-track player in it. This was before cassettes and CDs became popular. As a matter of fact, we didn't have an 8-track player in the house at this point, just in the car. I went to Dad and asked him for the keys to the car and explained that I wanted to listen to the Statler Brothers. He gave me the keys and off I went.

Here's a quick lesson about 8-track players of that day. They did not have a fast-forward or rewind. That meant you had to listen to every song in real time. The other thing about 8-track players is that they had four different stereo program sides that ten songs would be divided between—thus creating an 8-track.

Sometimes a song would start on one program side, fade out in the middle of the song, and then the player would change programs and pick the song up where it had left off on the next program. The one thing you could do was pick between the four different programs that had songs and with the click of the program button, you could change to a different program. Sounds complicated, doesn't it?

I went out to the car that day and put in the Statler Brothers 8-track. I knew every song by heart and I still do, but I was looking for "Susan When She Tried." When I found it, I listened very intently to how the song was put together. When the song was over, I had to wait for the program side to finish playing before I could switch back to hear the song again. I listened to that song over and over again.

I then went inside to my piano and began trying to play what I had heard. I had no written music. I just played by ear. When I would get stuck, I would head back out to the car and listen to the song again and again. What I didn't realize at the time was that I was teaching myself to play the piano by ear.

Before long, I moved on to the next song, and the next. I was practicing without anyone making me practice. I was enjoying the piano now because I was playing songs that I loved and wanted to sing. The Statler Brothers didn't know it, but their music inspired me to play the piano. After a short while, I went to Mom and asked her to find someone to give me piano lessons, but that this time I wanted to learn "real" songs.

She began searching for a teacher and finally found one... Jeff's mom, Gloria Duncan. The rest as they say, is history. I was now well on my way to becoming an accomplished piano player and this time it was because I wanted to.

When I sit down at the piano now, doing something that seems almost second-nature, I often think back to that watershed moment of my life, listening to the 8-track and then playing the piano. God was moving in my spirit. After all, I was simply following in the footsteps of those old-time Gospel greats, whose musical roots can be traced back at least 2,000 years, in Europe. We also read in Genesis 4 that one of the early patriarchs, Jubal, was the "father" of those of us who handle "the harp and organ."

It's easy to focus on the problems of life. The enemy wants you to feel defeated and that there is no hope. But oh my friend, God loves you and me so much. Those good seeds that I mentioned in the previous chapter are really there; it just takes time for them to grow.

An important lesson to learn is that you can walk away from a blessing if you're not careful. I could have given up and never touched a piano again and look at the blessing I would have lost out on. You must live your life having faith in God. Without faith, there is no hope. My faith started that fall of 1976, when I gave my heart and life to Jesus. When did your faith start? Have you given your heart and life to Jesus? If you haven't surrendered your life to Jesus, won't you do that right now by saying this simple prayer to Him?

"Dear Jesus, I know that I'm a sinner.

Please forgive me of my sins.

I believe that You died on a cross for me,

And I believe that You have risen from the dead.

Right now, I turn away from my sins

And I turn to You, I make You the Lord of my life.

Thank you for saving me,

And help me to tell someone right away

About my new decision."

If you said that prayer and you really meant it, let me be the first to say, "Welcome to the family of God!" This family doesn't care about what you've done in the past or if you're different. You've been saved. Go shout it from the rooftop. Lift your hand up and tell that fourth-grade class, "I've been saved!" Never be ashamed of what God has done for you. Get plugged into a Bible-believing church and get baptized. Find yourself a Bible and begin to read it and pray, just like my Uncle Gene did every day of his life. Only through Jesus can true happiness be found.

"I want to take away your pain

By giving you a joy like you've never known before

And all I ask is that you believe in Me

Turn from the darkness that doesn't want you to see

All I have to offer you starts at Calvary

The time is now so won't you believe?"

–Brian Arnold and Martha Jones
(From the song "Won't You Believe?")

Brian with
the
Southern Brothers

Brian with
Spoken 4 Quartet

Brian with
Todd Stewart
of
Compassion
International

"Friendship is born at that moment when one person says to another: What! You too? I thought I was the only one."

–C. S. Lewis

"There are "friends" who destroy each other, but a real friend sticks closer than a brother."
  Proverbs 18:24 (The New Living Translation)

Chapter Five

Friends

By 1981, I was most certainly ready to go to high school. In West Plains, the school system was made up of several elementary schools like Glenwood, but grades nine through twelve all came together in town. No longer would I be a Mustang, for now I would become a West Plains Zizzer. Many people have debated through the years as to just what is a Zizzer? Let me set the record straight right here and now. A Zizzer is simply... not a Whizzer (the junior high mascot). I hope that clears things up for you.

Glenwood had been an okay experience, but after my eighth-grade graduation ceremony I was ready to move on. Moving on meant going to a school where Dad was not the principal. I loved my dad, but I needed a change and high school represented just that...a change. I would now have seven different classes with seven different teachers, plus I got a locker to store my books and materials in. Dad still says that my locker saw more of my books than I did. One of my classes in high school didn't require any books at all and that class was my favorite—choir.

Choir opened up a whole new world to me, and one that changed my life in many ways. My choir director's name was Kelly Dame. She was definitely a very eccentric personality. I learned so much about singing and harmony from her, though. I guess part of it was that she made me feel important. I became the piano accompanist for all of Mrs. Dame's choirs and different ensemble groups, as well as all of the soloists going to local and state competitions from our school. Choir made me visible which was a different kind of feeling for me. Now don't mistake visible for popular. I was nowhere near being popular but visible was kind of nice.

In 1982, Mrs. Dame announced that the choir would be taking a trip to Great Britain in the summer of 1983. We began doing all kinds of fundraising to pay for the trip. We washed cars, picked up rocks, sold t-shirts, etc. You name it and we probably did it trying to earn money.

The city of West Plains really came together to help send us. This was the trip of a lifetime. Mom got to go as a sponsor as well. We toured all of England, Scotland and Wales, singing in all of the major cathedrals. We were in London during the celebration of the Queen's birthday and they were having a huge parade in her honor. There were horses and carriages everywhere and lots of pomp-and-circumstance.

And wouldn't you know that a small group of American kids would find themselves on a mostly vacant street at the very time Princess Diana and the Queen mother would be passing by in horse-drawn carriage with the top down on the way to take their place in the parade. We went crazy with excitement as she politely waved to us. I still have the photo that I took of her that day. Being overseas gave me a sense of wonder for the world that I live in. I have loved traveling ever since.

Although I have to admit that a big part of me would have loved to have been the school's star point guard, or quarterback, my experiences adapting to my disability led me to rich events such as the one I just described. The Apostle Paul admonishes us in Scripture to be content in all circumstances. It's good advice.

By 1982, Dad accepted a bi-vocational pastor's position at Berean Baptist Church, a little country church on the north side of West Plains. By now he had been preaching for a number of years but this was his first full-time position. This created quite a change for my family because we had to leave Bethel Baptist Church for good.

Now every Sunday morning and evening I would be the "preacher's kid," not just the occasional fill-in he had been up until then. This also included Wednesday night services and any other special services that might come up. The other thing I didn't see coming with Dad taking this position was the fact that I had to play the piano at church for most services, not to mention singing special music on a regular basis. When you're in high school, all you want to do is sit on the back row and be cool and playing the piano at church was not cool.

My mother was so proud at this point—she had bought that piano all of those years ago—and it was really paying off now. She would have me learn songs to sing at church, either as a solo or a duet with my sister Shelley, or occasionally as a family. Our family had two songs that were consistently requested, "Soon And Very

Soon" and "The Old Gospel Ship." My sister Amy never really enjoyed singing in front of people so I don't remember singing any duets with her. Mom's favorite song for me to sing though had to be "Sweet Beulah Land." She still insists that I sing that song today, every time I sing. There is such a comforting quality to this song, written in 1979 by Squire Parsons.

So we continued to transition into this new family role.

I am reminded of a story Dad says he doesn't recall, but believe me... I remember it very well. I was sitting on the back row at church minding my own business (talking with my friends), while Dad was up front behind the pulpit, preaching his sermon. I must not have been doing a very good job of concealing the fact that I wasn't paying attention to him because at one point Dad stopped his sermon and instructed me, in front of everyone in the church, to go sit by my mother. Needless to say, I was much more careful in the future.

This one small story, too, I think, reminds us that there has been such a culture-shift in America. Can you imagine a pastor (or, what do they call them today, "life coaches"?) calling-down an inattentive teen? I can't.

During these years, I became even more serious about my piano playing and decided to take classical training from the local concert pianist, Richard Trum. Mr. Trum was born in 1899 in St. Louis, Missouri, and lived right across the street from the high school. I could literally walk over there after school for my lessons. He was an elderly man whose house I remember to be very dark and musty. I'm not sure that I was ever allowed into any room other than the front room where the piano was located.

(An aside. Mr. Trum was a terrific teacher, but as I recall those days of lessons in his home, I laugh, remembering also the "Andy Griffith" episodes in which Barney Fife would take voice lessons from Mrs. Eleanora Poultice. Her star pupil had been Leonard Blush, and so she was always determined to shape Barney into a superstar in the style of Leonard Blush. Hopefully, the comparison ends there and I had more raw talent than Barney!)

Mr. Trum was very serious about classical music. He had obviously been around it all of his life. Even at his age, he could still play—by memory—many of the classical pieces beautifully. He taught me Chopin and Beethoven, Mozart and Rachmaninov, and many other classics. I remember looking at the twenty-six-page sheet music for Beethoven's "Moonlight Sonata" thinking, "How will I ever memorize all three movements?" I eventually did memorize it and many others.

Mr. Trum would often say to me, "I know it's written this way, but it was meant to be played like this." I suppose with all his experience, he understood the music better than anyone trying to put it in written form could. At one point during my training with him, he had me learn an all-left-handed piece. This had to be one of the hardest pieces of music I ever learned. I wasn't allowed to use my right hand at all, yet my left hand was all over the piano keys from one end to the other.

Who knew one day that one song would remind me that the piano could be played with one hand. Because of his teaching, I earned a scholarship to Southwest Missouri State University for classical piano. Thanks to him, I have a great love for classical music to this day. Richard Trum passed away on October 24, 1986.

When you learn my entire story, you'll have no trouble seeing the Hand of God in my life. The "left-handed" practice would prove to be a pivotal moment.

In high school, I made a number of friends to which I became very close. One of those friends was the boy I mentioned in the introduction of this book, Randall Lovelace. Randall was sort of an outcast like I was but for a totally different reason. Randall was an "in-your-face" type of Christian. He was bold with his faith and I was totally drawn to him because of it. He introduced me to Contemporary Christian music, mainly an artist by the name of Keith Green.

The first record of Keith's that I heard was called, "So You Wanna Go Back To Egypt?" I was hooked right away. His music was all piano-driven, as well as self-composed. Keith Green had a ministry called Last Days Ministries and they literally gave his albums away for whatever you could afford, plus they would send you a free monthly newsletter. This was music to my ears...free music!

Though now I'm older, I've gone back and purchased each CD at full price in an effort to repay his generosity.

Randall loved Gospel music as much as I did. I had seen the Blackwood Brothers sing at the fairgrounds there in West Plains and had been so inspired by them. I convinced Randall that we needed to start a quartet of our own. We enlisted the help of Kelly Hunter to sing bass and my buddy Jeff, the boy from Glenwood whose mother gave me piano lessons, to sing tenor. We called ourselves the Young Revelators.

We began practicing after school at Kelly's home church, the Church of God, and eventually starting booking ourselves at any place that would let us come sing. Dad even bought us a Peavey sound system to travel with. It was a four-channel board with four microphones and two speakers.

James Blackwood had really impacted me in a huge way. He was such a smooth singer and always dressed so sharply, especially when he wore an all-white suit. I remember telling Dad after seeing them in person that one day I wanted to be in a full-time Gospel quartet.

During my senior year of high school, my group went through some changes. Kelly had graduated the year before so we were no longer a quartet and Jeff had become very busy with other school activities, so Randall and I began the search for a new tenor singer. This is when I met a freshman named Ashley Ellison. Ashley and his family had recently moved from Willard, Missouri to West Plains.

Normally, seniors and freshmen are mortal enemies, but I had met Ashley in choir and began talking to him about singing with Randall and me. We auditioned him in the basement of his home around his mom's piano. Ashley couldn't sing by ear but he could read music and sing tenor very well. I look back at it now and I'm still amazed at the relationship I developed with him. Our age difference didn't matter at all and we quickly became best friends.

As my graduation drew closer, Ashley and his family moved back to Willard and although the Young Revelators never made it past high school, my dream of singing in a full-time gospel quartet would eventually come true. Who knew that it would include a lowly freshman?

Randall and I were also very good at getting into trouble together. Probably our favorite thing to do together outside of singing was "toilet-papering houses," otherwise known as TP-ing. This was a tradition of throwing toilet paper rolls into trees and was usually saved for Halloween night, but Randall and I took it to a totally new level and we didn't need the excuse of a holiday to do it either.

We would scale chimneys to wrap air vents, while leaving no column or bush without proper decoration. We were self-proclaimed masters who would strike without warning and leave without a sound—although we might leave a nametag!

One night after I was getting off work from the Nu-Way Grocery store, Randall and I headed off to create another masterpiece and I put my nametag in my coat pocket. It somehow fell out while we were working and the next day we got a call asking us to come clean up our "art." Randall never let me live that one down! One benefit to working at a grocery store though was getting toilet paper at a discount. We would buy it by the case.

Here's an interesting fact about the grocery store I worked at. "Preacher" Roe, the famous Dodgers' baseball pitcher, who lived in West Plains, originally owned it. I like to think he would have been proud of our "pitching motion" as we tossed toilet paper around town!

Randall and I also liked to skip school together to go fishing. Since Dad was no longer my principal, I felt I could get away with a *whole lot* more. I remember one time we skipped school to go fishing together, but it didn't turn out quite like I had planned.

I was careful to be back home at the appropriate time in order to not cause any suspicion, but for some reason Dad was particularly interested in how things had been at school that day. I tried to play it cool, but I knew something was wrong because he kept asking me more questions. He then went on to inform me that every day the high school sent Glenwood an attendance record of the students that came from their district and that for some reason he had decided to check it that particular day.

After an impressive lecture from Dad about skipping school, he told me that he would say nothing and just let the high school deal with my punishment if I got caught. The deal was, he made me promise not to sign his name to an excuse note. I made and kept that promise...it's just a good thing he didn't make me promise not to sign Mom's name to an excuse note!

There is one other day of skipping school with Randall that will live in infamy. Randall and I had waited until our senior year to take our one required science credit, General Science. We were the only two seniors in a class of mostly freshmen. Most kids took this class as freshmen and then they would go on to Biology and Chemistry the following years in preparation for college, but not Randall and I. We waited until we were in jeopardy of not graduating before taking a science class; besides, we were masters of the arts—music and TP-ing!

Anyway, at the beginning of the year, we were assigned a project as partners that required us to collect different leaves, identify them, store them in a book for a few weeks so that they would dry out and flatten, then assemble all of them together in a nice presentation. Being the science scholars that we were, Randall and I put the project off... until the day before it was due. We then elected to skip school...to go fishing, and oh by the way, collect leaves off of trees as Randall drove the car and I hung out the car window grabbing handfuls as we headed to the lake.

After a good day of fishing, Randall and I then went to visit his grandmother, who just happened to be an authority on leaves. After she had identified all of them for us, we headed back to Randall's house where we proceeded to dry them...in the microwave!

With our leaves now identified and dried, we assembled a very nice presentation and turned them in the next day. We received an A+ for our leaf presentation and our teacher praised our work in front of the whole class. Of course, she never knew the true story. I only share this story now because the statute of limitations must surely be up!

It was during my high school years that I started writing songs. The first song I ever wrote was a simple melody on the piano that I thought sounded nice. I found out later that it was really "Color My World" by Chicago. This didn't deter me from writing, though. I found writing to be an outlet for the emotions I was hiding inside. Most people never knew what I really thought about myself because I didn't share those kinds of feelings with anyone, including my parents.

I began to write love songs for all the girls I would fall in love with, yet I would never share the songs with anyone except Randall, Ashley or Tom Seeley, another boy who I met in school that shared an interest in singing and writing. I was scared to death of girls and I never had a girlfriend while I was in high school, but I wrote songs for many of them that went unheard. I was in love with one girl named Carrie almost all throughout high school. She was a cheerleader and I was in choir with her. She was quite popular and I was quite the opposite.

I wrote a song in honor of her that I simply titled, "Carrie." Randall and Tom used to encourage me to say something to her, but I couldn't. There was no way she was interested in me, a boy with one leg who wasn't in the "in" crowd. After high school, I finally mustered up the courage to send her some roses with a note asking her out. She was very sweet to me, but I never got the date and she never heard the song.

I was lonely throughout most of high school, always longing to have a girlfriend. Oh, I had friends, just no girlfriend. In my mind it was always because of my leg. As I look back now, I realize that a poor self-image will never be attractive to anyone. I never believed in myself at all when it came to relationships. In my mind, I was still that little boy that was tormented for having a "wooden" leg. Yet I thank God to this day for Randall, Ashley and Tom. They helped me through some lonely days and nights.

The sad thing was, I never realized at the time that they accepted me for who I was. And in spite of the mischief I got into with Randall, he was still one of those "good seeds" that God planted in my life. Unfortunately, I was on a path that saw only the "bad seeds."

What path are you on today? Have you allowed the enemy to keep you from seeing the "good seeds" God has planted in your life? Despite how your life has turned out so far, Jesus wants to be your friend. He'll be closer than a brother if you let Him. I made the mistake of not letting Him be my best friend and eventually my other friends couldn't ease my inner pain and I would go on to make some tragic errors in judgment.

Don't fall into that same trap that I did. Turn to Jesus right now and let Him show you the life He intends for you to have. You'll never create the life you want on your own. Only God can give you what you truly need. Let Jesus be your best friend today.

"I can't see Him but I can feel Him all around

I know He's there, everywhere

Somebody's watchin' me"

–Brian Arnold and Chresten Tomlin
(From the song "Somebody's Watchin' Me")

Kelsey and Josh,
Bella and Cruz
The Keeton Family

Brian's grandson, Cruz

Cruz and Bella

Brian's granddaughter, Bella

"Going to church doesn't make you a Christian any more than standing in a garage makes you a car."

—Anonymous

"For wisdom is a defense... but the excellency of knowledge is, that wisdom giveth life to them that have it."

Ecclesiastes 7:12 (KJV)

Chapter Six

A Snowball...

After high school graduation I attended one semester of college at Southwest Missouri State University in West Plains before moving to Springfield, Missouri to attend at the main campus. I decided against living on campus because of my leg. I wanted more privacy than a college dorm room would provide, so I moved in with Ashley and his folks in Willard for awhile until Dad came to my rescue and helped me get into a little apartment located behind a Steak 'n Shake restaurant. It was a nice place, especially for being my first home away from home.

I got a job at Hanger Prosthetics working with Bob Busbee. Hanger Prosthetics was where artificial legs and arms were made and Bob had made several of my legs through the years. At one point while I was working there, I actually made my own leg (with a lot of help from Bob).

Looking back now at this next period of my life, I can see where the enemy's noose began to tighten around me, but at the time I had no idea what was about to happen in my life. I was in desperate need of validation and especially from a female. My high school years had been filled with unfulfilled dreams of finding someone to love me and now that I was living on my own, this need was even more prevalent. For the first time in my life I was really alone.

My family was two hours away and my only friend in the Springfield area was in high school. I wanted a girlfriend. I *needed* a girlfriend. "I'm nineteen! I should practically be married by now!" or so I thought.

Ashley invited me to attend his home church. Before this time, I had never even given any thought to choosing a church to attend. I had just always attended where my folks went. I knew I needed to go, so I accepted his invitation and joined him one night. That one night would start a chain of events that would forever change my life.

That night I met "the one," the girl I'd been looking for. I'm going to refer to her as "Sue", because in no way do I want her to be unfairly judged. She has her own side to this story and her own reasons for why things happened the way that they did. I'm going to try and tell this story from my point of view, focusing mainly on my own failures without casting blame on her. In the end, our lives are what we make of them. I can't blame someone else for why my life didn't turn out the way I wanted it to.

I went to church that night with Ashley with really no expectations one way or the other. It was just church. I wish I had been more diligent about why I was going to church instead of just going out of some sense of obligation. I knew it was important to God that I was there, but I hadn't yet realized the importance it should have to me personally. I can't tell you anything about the service that night. My only memory is of meeting Sue for the first time. I remember walking into the hallway that led to the downstairs classrooms and seeing this beautiful girl crying in the office. She caught my eye right away. My heart went out to her immediately. I don't think she even knew I was there. She was talking with the pastor and so I continued on downstairs.

I located Ashley and began describing to him the girl I had just seen. I wanted to know who she was and why she was upset. He told me that she was the pastor's daughter. My interest was really peaked now because I'm a pastor's son and the thought of hooking up with someone like myself was very intriguing. This girl had to have similar struggles coping with being a "PK," preacher's kid. I asked Ashley to introduce me to her after church.

I can still remember talking to Sue for the first time on the sidewalk outside of the church. She was so sweet. I didn't ask her why she had been crying, although I would find out much later. She seemed interested in me as I told her a little about myself. Of course, I told her I was also a PK and we laughed about how difficult that could be at times. I also told her about my leg. I'm sure I made some joke about it. I figured I might as well get it out in the open right from the start. This would surely turn her off... but it didn't even seem to faze her.

She just kept smiling at me and as the night drew to a close I finally mustered up the courage to ask her for her phone number. This was a big step for me, I promise you. I had never had much self-confidence around girls, but there was something different about Sue. We seemed to connect right away. I must have grinned the whole way back home after she consented to giving me her number.

My brain went into overdrive about Sue. Suddenly I couldn't do anything but think about her. This girl was actually interested in me. Ashley advised me to play it cool and not call her the minute I got home. One thing Ashley didn't have trouble with was girls. He was very popular at school and always had girls calling him, so I decided to trust him and I waited until the next day to call Sue. I didn't want to mess this up!

My first mistake was not getting advice from the Lord. Isn't this a common problem for all of us? Don't misunderstand me, Sue was a good person, but I don't believe I once asked God for His opinion on anything to do with her. I just assumed she was His answer to my problems. Too often we get ahead of God. I knew I was lonely and I wanted a girlfriend, so I moved heaven and earth to have one.

I called Sue the next day and asked her out for a date. She said yes and I was crazy with delight. God *had* to be in this. I couldn't wait. I was nervous but charged with excitement when I picked her up at her home. She lived right next door to the church, in the parsonage. We were going bowling together. After leaving her parents' home, she asked if I minded to stop by a local pizza parlor for her to see her best friend for a moment. I was eager to please her so I said yes. I remember waiting on her for quite some time not really knowing what they were talking about. Again, I would find out later.

After bowling, we stopped at the Steak 'n Shake by my apartment for a quick bite to eat and then we headed to my place. I was incredibly nervous with Sue being at my apartment. I wanted to be a gentleman and play it cool, but my mind was overloaded with all kinds of thoughts.

"Should I sit next to her? Should I put my arm around her? Should I have soft music playing? Should I kiss her?" My mind was racing in every direction. We eventually ended up sitting on the floor talking and listening to the soundtrack album to "Top Gun."

Not surprisingly, "Heaven In Your Eyes" became *our* song, and that was exactly what I saw in Sue's eyes that night as I kissed her for the very first time...heaven. To say I fell in love instantly would probably be an understatement. I had never felt so much for any one person before and to think, she really liked me. That was the icing on the cake. I had fallen in love with girls before but only from a distance. This girl knew I had an artificial leg and it didn't bother her at all. She actually cared that I existed.

Sue was a senior in high school and I was busy attending Southwest Missouri State College working on my music degree. Classes were very boring to me because I was in love and that consumed me. She was the answer, not school. I had been classically trained on the piano in high school, so the beginning college courses for music were a bit elementary for me and this added to my distaste for college.

My folks had pushed me so hard to go into education because there was financial security there, but I didn't listen. I would spend hours every day in one of the piano practice rooms writing songs. I was supposed to be practicing my classical music, but the solitude seemed better-spent writing of my love for Sue. I had many a concert by myself in those piano rooms. I know the other students had to be wondering what class I was taking. I know my parents did.

I couldn't wait to see Sue the first time I wrote her a song. Since she lived right next to the church, I asked her dad if I could take her over to the sanctuary and play it for her. He said yes and I'll never forget her response. She just couldn't believe it. She told me that no one had ever done anything like that for her before. I felt like a million bucks.

This was the first time I had ever written a love song for someone that I could honestly say I was in love with. She sat right next to me on the piano bench as I serenaded her. It was like right out of a movie. I just knew God had brought her to me. I thanked Him for her every day.

It wasn't long after we started dating that Sue and I began to have sex. I totally disregarded everything I knew to be right, because I was in love. I justified everything, as "this was God's plan for my life." I felt that I had suffered enough in my life and this was God's way of making it up to me.

Let me just say that I know now that God will never bless you with something that is contrary to His Word, but at the time I refused to see it or even consult Him on the matter. I was totally consumed with what I wanted, not what God wanted. No one had any idea of what kind of relationship Sue and I were having. It was our little secret. I pursued Sue like no other. I was obsessed with her, really. I would get up early each school morning and drive to her house to be the one to wake her up. I would then sit and wait on her, as she got ready for school. Then I would drive her to school and drop her off. I wanted everyone to know that she was taken.

After she got out of school, she would catch a ride to work. Just as soon as I could get off work myself, I would drive to the restaurant where she worked, and sit and wait for her shift to be over. Then we would spend the evening together until she had to go to bed. This happened almost every day. I couldn't get enough of her and all the while I was always afraid that it would be over, that she would change her mind about me. I was totally unprepared to be in a relationship, especially one where sex was involved.

As we continued to date, I began to find out why Sue had been crying the night I met her. That night her father had just forbidden her to have anything to do with her boyfriend. I'll call him Joe. Apparently he was regarded as trouble by her parents and they didn't want her around him. I guess they approved of me because I was a "good" boy. I'm sure they would have changed their opinion of me if they had really known what was going on.

This knowledge that Sue had been forced to end her relationship with Joe just added to my fears. Suddenly, everything seemed too good to be true. I also found out later that the reason Sue had asked me to stop and see her friend the night of our first date, was so that she could check on Joe.

I began to live in fear while still being totally obsessed with Sue. I suppose a "normal" person would have bailed out, realizing that her heart was really somewhere else, but I couldn't bring myself to believe that. The fact was that I was afraid to go back to being alone, so I hid my head in the sand and hoped for the best.

Then I got the idea to propose to Sue. This would end all of my doubts if she said yes to my proposal. Besides, I was in love with her and I wanted to spend the rest of my life with her. I proposed to Sue one night while standing out back of her house. To my surprise, she said yes. This was music to my ears. I told myself to quit worrying about Sue's feelings for Joe and just be happy. *"God's in control of all of this,"* I told myself.

I called my Grandma Oma and explained to her that I was ready to marry Sue, but that I couldn't afford an engagement ring for her. Grandma came through for me and gave me the money. I then went to Sue's dad to ask for his daughter's hand in marriage. I just knew that he would be as excited as I was, but I was wrong. I'll never forget sitting in his office listening to him tell me that his daughter was not right for me and that he wouldn't recommend my following through with marrying her. I couldn't believe what I was hearing. Unfortunately, this just encouraged me even more. *"How could a father say things like that about his daughter?"* I thought.

I see now that he could see the bigger picture and I couldn't. He realized that she wasn't ready for marriage and frankly, neither was I, but no one could have told me any different. This was a "God" thing.

Boy, was I wrong.

Not long after we were engaged Sue became pregnant. No one but she and I knew. I took her to the doctor and it was confirmed. This didn't faze me at all. I was in love. I thought to myself, *"We're already married in God's eyes just not in man's,"* so I didn't think another thing about it. We still didn't tell anyone the truth, though.

This should have been a big sign that God wasn't pleased. God never condones sin under any circumstance. Our happiness is not a reason to justify sin, yet I thought it was. I had myself convinced that everything was going according to God's plan. Little did I know that the snowball was just beginning to go downhill.

Friend, don't ever put your happiness above what God wants. Proverbs 15:21 says, "Folly is joy to him that is destitute of wisdom, but a man of understanding walketh uprightly." (KJV) I can see now that I didn't use the wisdom Sue's dad tried to give me. Oxford's American Dictionary defines folly as "a lack of good sense."

Listen, King Solomon wrote many of the proverbs, and he eventually found out what his father, David, knew: life will teach you. Boy, will it. In my mind's eye, I can see David and Solomon, at the end of each of their lives, huddled by a fire in the palace, lamenting the many poor choices they'd made in life. I wish young people were taught to understand where these men were in their lives, and then to really meditate on their excellent wisdom.

So, Proverbs teaches us that a lack of good sense will only make you think you're happy when you choose not to listen to God. Don't ever get ahead of God. Learn to wait on Him and when He knows you're truly ready for the next step in your life, He'll lead you to it.

"Carrying my own cross, serving my cause

Proudly proclaiming all that I thought I was

But my good intentions couldn't erase anything

It took a blood spattered cross that once held a King"

–Brian Arnold and Martha Jones
(From the song "My Good Intentions")

Brian with his
personal assistant,
Betty Hastings
and friend,
David Fountain

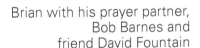

Diane, Kerrigan, David and Kelsey

Brian with his prayer partner,
Bob Barnes and
friend David Fountain

Guess who is
coming to town?
Brian performing
with daughters,
Kelsey and Kerrigan,
and friend David

"When life gives you lemons, you might just end up with a sour look on your face. Sometimes there just aren't any easy answers and nothing can be said."

-Brian Arnold

"A man reaps what he sows."

Gal. 6:7

Chapter Seven

Headed For Hell....

One of the most carnal music acts in history, AC/DC, often writes and performs songs that tell the story of a man bound for hell...and he knows it. Certainly, one can wonder just what their first front-man, Ronald Belford "Bon" Scott, thought about his decadent lifestyle just after he died prematurely at age 33.

The fact that Sue was now pregnant never bothered me, because I was living the dream. But it did begin to bother her. I look back now and I can only imagine what she was living with. The simple truth was that she loved both of us in different ways and she was way too young to know how to deal with all these emotions and should never have had to deal with any of this, anyway. It was totally unfair of me to pressure her the way that I did. I never gave her a moment away from me to even think things through. Of course in my defense, I wasn't facing reality. Remember, my head was in the sand hoping for the best. There have been so many times since then that I wish I had handled things differently. So much for being the perfect gentleman...

I should have known that Sue wasn't dealing with this very well the day she came to me and asked to borrow my car to go see Joe. She explained to me that since we were getting married soon, she needed to give him back his things that he had given her and get some of her things back as well. This seemed like a reasonable request at the time. I knew her dad would be upset, but I wanted her to have closure with Joe. I reasoned in my mind that if she saw him one last time, it would be over and we could move on. What happened next still seems surreal even after all these years.

Sue took me to work that day and headed off to see Joe. Yes, I was nervous, but I trusted her...*didn't I?* Several hours went by and it seemed like the longest day of my life. My mind was racing with thoughts.

Would she see him and decide she was still in love with him or would they get into an argument and he hurt her?

What was taking her so long?

Did she break down in my car or did he kidnap her?

What were they doing together that was taking this much time?

Why wasn't she back yet?

Finally, she showed up at my job and I immediately knew something was wrong. She was obviously in shock about something that had happened. I tried to get her to tell me but she refused. She didn't seem to be in any frame of mind to be alone, so I went to my boss and explained the situation to him. He allowed me to take off early from work so that I could take her back to my apartment and figure out what was wrong.

My apartment was only a couple of miles away and I rushed to get her there so that I could start getting to the bottom of what was going on. Sue hardly said a word the entire ride. I could tell that she had been crying and I began to hurt all over for her.

When we arrived at my apartment, I quickly jumped out and opened her car door and helped her to the door. I unlocked my apartment, opened the door and stepped back to let her go in first. As she walked in I noticed dirt on the back of her pink sweater. There were even some loose grass clippings still clinging to it. Now I definitely knew something bad had happened.

I got Sue inside and tried everything I knew to get her to confide in me, yet all the while in the back of my mind a fear was growing. It wasn't until hours later that I found out the truth. This truth would forever change my world. The fear that had been growing in the back of my mind was now raging as Sue finally said, *"I was raped by Joe."*

Even now, reliving this moment of my life still hurts me to the core. At that very moment, my world began to crumble right in front of me. Joe had always been my nemesis, even though we had never met in person. Now, this man was my enemy because he had hurt the one girl who had shown me any kind of love.

Sue was hurting and nothing I could do seemed to help. I was filled with rage, yet crying so hard I could barely see. I wanted to call the police but Sue was emphatic: *"No!"* She didn't want the police to tell her dad what had happened. She made me promise not to tell them. She begged me not tell her father. At that very moment I would have done anything she asked of me. All I wanted to do was take away her pain.

This is my fault!

I should have never let her take my car to go see him!

Thought after thought raged through my mind. I wanted Joe beat to the point of death. I wanted him thrown in jail and the key to be thrown away. I wanted to hurt him like he had hurt Sue. I wanted to hurt him like he had hurt me. I was devastated. All I could do was sit with my hand on her shoulder. She didn't want to be touched... even by me.

Nothing was really said on the car ride back to her house. She just kept repeating, *"Don't tell Dad. Please, don't tell my dad."*

When we got back to her house she insisted on walking in alone. I know she must have been trying to keep me from her parents, in fear that I might break my promise. There was no hug, no kiss... only me saying through tear-filled eyes, *"I love you, Sue. God, I love you. I'm so sorry..."*

She said nothing and just turned and walked into the house. I sat in the car with my heart breaking into a million pieces and there wasn't anything that I could do to stop it from happening. I couldn't even pray. I felt totally helpless. The car ride home was the loneliest car ride of my life.

Several days went by. I lived in utter torment. I had heard about hell all of my life and I was sure that the way I was feeling had to be as close as you could possibly get to hell here on Earth.

Sue didn't want to see me and barely talked to me on the phone. This only worsened my fragile state of mind. I hadn't told anyone what had happened. I was bearing all this by myself. Even Sue didn't want me around, let alone us talk about it in fear that someone might overhear our conversation. Yet I had to tell someone. Joe could *not* go unpunished. He had ruined our lives with his act of selfishness. I was like Al Pacino's unhinged character in "Scarface," Tony Montana.

Sue had made me promise not to go to the police or to tell her dad what had happened, but she didn't say anything about not telling her older brother. I barely even knew him because he didn't live at home anymore and his relationship with his parents was strained, but I knew he loved his sister and that he hated Joe. I called him from work about a week after the assault and broke down in tears over the phone telling him what had happened. I wanted Joe hurt and in a bad way. God forgive me for those awful things that I thought and said about him. Sue's brother assured me that he would deal with the situation.

I showed up at Sue's house later that same day and was met by her father at the door. He informed me that I was not allowed to see her anymore. Apparently, Sue's brother had gone straight to their father with the information I had given him.

This isn't what I wanted to have happen!

I just wanted justice against Joe. I looked at Sue's father and said, *"How can you keep me away from her at a time like this? I love Sue. Please don't shut me out."* He then when on to inform me that they had taken Sue to the emergency room for tests and you can just imagine what they found...Sue was pregnant. Of course, this was no surprise to me but I immediately realized that she hadn't told her parents the truth. I stood there speechless.

I know her father must have thought that I was reeling from the news of his daughter's pregnancy, but in fact I was at a loss for words because she hadn't told them that I was the father. I left Sue's house in complete confusion. I didn't know up from down. I didn't know what to say or do.

Later that night, I got a call from Sue asking me to come over for a moment. *Finally...a ray of sunshine.* She must have told her Dad how much she loved and needed me, and he consented to let me come over. I quickly jumped into my car and raced over to Sue's house.

She was waiting outside on the porch for me. I was so glad to see her. It had been over a week since I had last been with her. I couldn't wait to wrap my arms around her and tell her that I loved her and that everything would be okay. I also wanted to talk to her about the confusion her parents had concerning her pregnancy.

As I got out of my car and began walking towards her, the look on her face told me something was very wrong. I attempted to hug her, but she brushed me away and told me that we needed to talk. In her hand she held the engagement ring that I had borrowed money from my grandmother to purchase for her. She took my hand and placed the ring in it and began telling me about how this was a very confusing time for her.

She told me that this was only temporary, just until she could work through everything that had just happened to her. I began to cry. She went on to say that she was sorry but that there was just too much going on right now and that she needed some time alone. What could I say?

I forgot all about asking her anything concerning the pregnancy. I was stunned. The conversation was short and to the point. She turned and went back inside. I didn't know it at the time, but it would be years before I ever saw her beautiful face again. Later that same night she called and informed me that it was really over and that she had not had the heart to tell me the truth in person.

As for me...I said nothing to anyone. I had never been so hurt in all my life. Joe had taken everything from me. I couldn't even think about the pregnancy. I had now lost everything that mattered to me.

I quit college and moved back home with my parents for a while. I couldn't even bring myself to tell them the truth. Sue called me one time after that night just to check in on me. I'm not really sure why she did that. Guilt maybe...I don't know. I still said nothing. I kept everything inside.

I know this may be hard to believe, but it gets worse. I found out later, that Sue had moved out and moved in with Joe's parents. As unbelievable as that may seem, she and Joe were soon married. He joined the military and they left the state together. It would be over five years before I would ever hear anything else about Sue and Joe. My heart was now completely destroyed.

I wish I had something real spiritual to tell you right now, but I don't. The best advice I can give you is that if you build your house on sand, expect a storm to eventually wash it away. This doesn't mean that God doesn't still love you, but He may choose not to save you from the consequences of your sin.

"Our Father who art in heaven,

Hallowed be Thy name

Thy Kingdom come, Thy will be done

On earth as it is in heaven

Give us this day our daily bread

And forgive us our trespasses...."

–Jesus Christ

Brian with author, Kevin Malarkey

Brian in Ecuador with Samaritan's Purse

Brian's daughter, Kerrigan

Kelsey singing at TCT

Kerrigan and David

"Even though you may want to move forward in your life, you may have one foot on the brakes."

–Mary Manin Morrissey

"Father, I have sinned against heaven and against you. I am no longer worthy to be called your son."

Luke 15:21

Chapter Eight

Running From God

Life without Sue was very difficult for me. I was tormented with thoughts of guilt and anger, but mostly inadequacy. What was wrong with me? Why had Sue done the unthinkable and married Joe? Was I really that bad of a choice? My parents really never fully understood my grief, but how could they? I was not completely honest with them about what had happened. Advice is never really good advice unless you're completely honest about your problem.

I should have been in counseling, but instead I hid the truth.

In 1987, I got a call from my former high school music teacher, Mrs. Dame, asking me if I would accompany her and her choir to Austria and Hungary that upcoming summer. Of course, I accepted the offer because being in a foreign country sounded like being far away from my problems. On my last trip out of the country my mother had gone with me. This time, I was a chaperone and my younger sister, Shelley, who was still in school was going.

It was a good trip, although if I had been in a better frame of mind, it would have been better. The castles in Hungary were actually more stunning than those I had seen in Great Britain. Austria was wonderful as well. I still picture it in my mind every time I watch "The Sound Of Music."

Still though, being in Austria and Hungary didn't take me away from the pain of losing Sue and the guilt of her pregnancy.

When I returned to the United States, I moved to Osage Beach, Missouri, and started working for Mark Sexton's Starworld Showroom. Osage Beach was a smaller version of Branson, Missouri. Mark was a musician who had moved in from Laughlin, Nevada to start a music show. It was Vegas Meets the Ozarks. Lots of glitz and laser lights with country music peppered in for good measure. My buddy, Ashley, had moved there for the summer to work at another music show and he had encouraged me to audition for this one.

The irony in all of this was that I had auditioned for the show he was in back before my breakup, and I had actually been offered a position as the show's piano player.

Of course, I turned the job down because I was in love with Sue, so I told Ashley about a job opportunity there as a horn player. His parents were going through a divorce at the time, so when he got the job, he decided to live with his uncle for the summer just to get away from things for awhile. After moving to Osage Beach, he learned that there was an opening at Mark's show, so he called me.

Working in a music show was worlds away from any life I had ever known. I was wearing spandex shirts and glitter coats while playing trumpet and keyboards. All I had ever performed my entire life was gospel music and classical piano pieces.

Now I was playing Charlie Daniels and Nitty Gritty Dirt Band music, along with a host of other artists. I was now in a band. I had never played in a band before. Most of these guys were seasoned musicians. I was totally out of place. Mark really encouraged me during this time of my life though. I began to write songs about my feelings of losing Sue, and when I wasn't performing the show, I sat out by the pool at my apartment and wrote songs in my head.

Ashley and I eventually moved in together. I know this had to be hard on him at times because I wasn't a happy person to be around. I finally broke down one night and bared my soul to him. He felt sorry for me and tried to encourage me to move on with my life, but as with any seventeen-year-old, his attention span was limited.

He was always dating someone new that he had met at the show and I was always the depressing guy he lived with. I never went out on dates or even thought about asking anyone out. I just knew that no one wanted me. I was so beaten-down mentally by this point that no one was going to cheer me up for long.

Ashley and I ended up inviting another friend of ours to move in with us. His name was Eric Shertz. Eric was a handsome kid that could really play the trumpet well. The three of us lived in a one-bedroom apartment. Sometimes being at home was like being at the zoo. Eric and Ashley always had friends over and were going here and there, all the time.

I went to work and sat by the pool. That was it. At one point we had a short-lived gospel trio called the "Osage Beach Boys." Pretty original huh?! It didn't last very long, though, because Ashley and Eric were always on-the-go.

One night during one of my performances, I did meet a girl from Chicago and for the first time since my breakup I was drawn to someone else. She had caught my eye during the first half of the show, so I rushed out to find her at intermission. She seemed very nice and interested in me so after the show was over I decided to step out of my comfort zone and ask her out.

Ashley was always encouraging me to do that, so this time I took his advice. The problem was, she was leaving to go back to Chicago early the next morning, so her parents thought it wouldn't be a very good idea for her to be out late. We exchanged phone numbers and addresses though.

I never saw her again after that night, but we had the most wonderful long-distance relationship possible. At one point we even talked about getting married. Crazy talk I know, but she was sweet and I was desperate for any kind of female attention. I didn't realize it at the time, but I was really just trying to replace what I had with Sue. This would become a common theme in my life.

After my first year in Osage Beach, I was offered another year's contract but this time I would be the featured piano player. Up until then, I had been a secondary keyboard player who played string and horn lines and occasionally played a note or two on the trumpet. This was quite an honor, because the man I replaced was an incredible musician who had left the show to return to Las Vegas. My life again was about to change.

Before my second season in Osage Beach started, I went back home to West Plains. I met a girl named Cindy and we instantly began a relationship. It wasn't too long after we started dating that I moved back to Osage Beach into a two-bedroom apartment with another friend. Fearful that the distance between us would break us apart, I suggested to her that she move in with me for the summer. This was a really bad idea, not because Cindy was a bad person, but because it was wrong. Once again, I ignored the way God said to do things because I had tunnel vision.

My happiness was of utmost importance to me. What I didn't take into consideration was that it was also of utmost importance to God. His way would have taken longer but would have resulted in true happiness. My way was quicker happiness followed by lots of unhappiness. I didn't see my unhappiness right away, but in time I was very unhappy and didn't know why.

My second season in Osage Beach was exciting but at the same time unfulfilling. Talk about confusion. I thought, *"I should be happy!"* I was now the featured piano player and Mark was giving me singing features as well. At one point, he had me dressed as a cowboy impersonating Hank Williams. I'm not sure that up to that point in my life I had even heard a Hank Williams song, but here I was singing "Lovesick Blues" and yodeling too! To be honest...I was an awful Hank Williams impersonator.

By the end of the 1988 season I was frustrated, angry and depressed. Cindy and I left Osage Beach and headed for Branson. Her mother had taken a job at the local Wal-Mart and Branson seemed as good a place to go as any.

Most people know Branson as the "Live Music Show Capital of the World," but I didn't move there with dreams of joining a show. No,

I went there running from God and ended up working in the toy department at Wal-Mart.

I can tell you from my personal experience that you won't find happiness in life in the toy department of a Wal-Mart unless you are under the age of ten! What you get instead is lots of screaming kids messing up the shelves that you've spent hours straightening. Parents think that dropping their kids off in the toy department is some form of childcare.

My career was now going nowhere and so was my relationship with Cindy and with God. I was depressed thinking about what my life was supposed to have been like with Sue and what our family would have been like. Then one day, a co-worker invited me to a revival meeting. He explained that in his life outside of Wal-Mart he was a preacher. God immediately began working on me. I wanted to say no and avoid the guilt of my lifestyle but my friend kept encouraging me to come out one night.

I don't remember what the name of the church was or what my friend preached about, but I do remember God firmly getting my attention. I went to the altar that night and rededicated my life to the Lord. The presence of the Holy Spirit came over me like I had never felt before. I left that church determined to clean my life up. I ended my relationship with Cindy, got my own apartment and started attending church regularly.

God is never really as far away as you might think He is. His desire is to mend broken fellowship. In Luke 15, we read the story of the Prodigal's son. Here's a guy who had it all but wanted more. He came to his father and demanded his inheritance and left to pursue his own idea of happiness. As we all know, he ended up with the pigs. When he got so far down, he remembered what he once had back with his father, and headed for home. Luke 15:20 says, "... **but while he was still a long way off**, *his father saw him and was filled with compassion for him; he ran to his son, threw his arms around him and kissed him.*"

What a beautiful picture! You may be a long way from home, but when you turn to head back, your Father sees you, because He's watching for your return. He's longing for your return. One of my favorite songs is "When God Ran" by Phillips, Craig and Dean, and it says the only time you'll ever see God run is when He's running to you. If you've wandered away from the path God had intended for you to be on, turn around! He's watching for your return and He'll start running to you.

"You say your feet won't take you farther

You say you're giving up that you can't go on

But there is a river, an unending oasis of love

It has a special name, that name is Jesus

Come sit at His feet again"

–Brian Arnold and Chresten Tomlin
(From the song "Come Sit At His Feet")

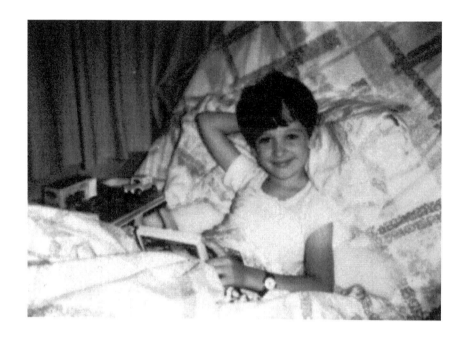

(1973) Brian in the hospital after losing his leg

Brian and sister Shelley with his grandparents, Glendon & Oma Arnold

(1983) Brian and his mother, Shirley at Stonehenge

(1985) Brian with his family - sisters Amy & Shelley,
parents, Shirley & Bob Arnold

(1986) Brian with his piano teacher, Richard
Trum (pictured with another student)

(1991) Brian with the Time Machine Band at Silver Dollar City

(1992) Chosen Few at Silver Dollar City - Ashley, Terry, Brian and Ray

(1993) Chosen Few at Silver Dollar City - David, Jody, Ashley & Brian
(Forest on upright bass)

(1994) Brian in
the halo brace

Brian's parents, Bob & Shirley
Arnold

(1994) Chosen Few - Scott, David, Ashley & Brian

(2000) Brian with Chosen Few at Silver Dollar City's
Echo Hollow Amphitheater

(2001) Chosen Few - Brian, Casey, Scott & Ashley

(2005) Brian's ordination - Pastor Tim Brooks,
Christian Ministries Church, Hot Springs, AR

Band of Brothers - Jerry, Dan, Pat and Brian

(2009) Brian with Mincaye in Ecuador
(also pictured is Mincaye's wife and grandson)

(2009) Brian and daughter Kerrigan singing at The Villages, FL.

(2010) Voices of Glory singing on Brian's Christmas Show for TCT.

(2010) Brian with daughter Kelsey while filming Brian's
Christmas Show for TCT

Brian and Franklin Graham

Brian with Don Piper, author of "90 Minutes in Heaven

Eric Hinson & Hinson Revival on the set of Brian's TCT show,
"From Victim To Victory"

Brian with Dottie Rambo (also pictured is Roy Sharpe)

Brian with Charlie Daniels

Brian and Don Reid of the Statler Brothers

Brian's
road manager
Dan Lyming

Brian with his
friend Don Enz

Brian's ministry coordinator and dear
friend, Betty Hastings

Brian's armor bearer and
prayer partner, Bob Barnes.

(2011) Brian co-hosting TCT Today with
Julie Nolan (left) and Marcie Wahl

(2010) Brian's twin boys - Austin and Justin

Brian's Uncle
Gene Horn

Brian's kids - Justin, Kelsey (top)
Kerrigan & Austin

(1994) First wedding picture
–Kelsey, Diane & Brian

(1994) Second wedding picture
–Diane & Brian

Brian's granddaughter, Bella on the set of his TCT Christmas Show

Brian's grandson, Cruz

"You gain strength, courage, and confidence by every experience in which you really stop to look fear in the face. You are able to say to yourself, 'I have lived through this horror. I can take the next thing that comes along.'"

–Eleanor Roosevelt

"He who conceals his sins does not prosper, but whoever confesses and renounces them finds mercy."

Proverbs 28:13 (NIV)

Chapter Nine

There's No Business Like Show Business

Now that I felt like things were getting back on track with God, I started evaluating my life. I was still not facing any of my past mistakes concerning Sue, but instead, looking for a new band-aid for my heart. I missed being "in love." I felt cheated by what had happened and now I had a new mission: *"I need to be married!"* Makes perfect sense doesn't it? NO!!!!

You see...by not dealing with the past correctly, I doomed my future. I had learned a valuable lesson with Cindy—don't live with someone you're not married to. God doesn't like that. But what I didn't learn was that I needed to come clean about my past. No, instead I headed out to find Ms. Right, right now, and boy, was she in trouble.

I was still working at Wal-Mart trying to get my life together when I noticed a pretty redhead named Patty working in women's clothing. So what's a guy from the toy department doing in women's clothing? *(That's a bad joke, I know...)*

Patty was a sweet, Christian girl who was very reserved and quiet. I began to make frequent trips to the women's clothing department just to say hi or ask how she was doing that day. She *thought* she saw me coming and tried to keep things slow, but I was a man on a mission. The sad thing was though; Patty *didn't* see me coming the way she thought she did. I never shared any of my past with her. I just tried to come off as this nice Christian guy who was ready to settle down. I really thought that was who I was.

I had the full-court pressure on too! It wasn't long before I began proposing marriage. Patty tried to take it slow and she refused my offers, but this only motivated me more. I wanted to be married. I wanted the life I had been cheated out of and I had convinced myself that this was God's will for us to be married.

Eventually, Patty accepted my proposal and we were married in a nice church wedding in Branson, but in the pit of my stomach something was very wrong. Of course, I ignored God trying to get my attention, because I was on my way to the life I had dreamed of, the life I felt I deserved after everything that had happened to me...the life I had convinced myself that God was pleased with.

In 1989, while still working at Wal-Mart, I got a call from Brandi Chapman, one of my friends I had worked with in Osage Beach. She had recently moved to Branson and was getting ready to audition for a show at Silver Dollar City, a local theme park. She asked me if I would play the piano for her audition and I gladly agreed to help.

Sitting in the audience the day of the audition was a guy named Gene Mulvaney. I didn't know Gene but he would soon get to know me.

A week or so later, I was hard at work (babysitting) in the toy department when a man asked me who I was. After I told him, he introduced himself to me as Gary Wilkinson. Gary was one of three brothers who had started a very successful show in Branson back in the early '80s. He explained that Gene had seen me at an audition and told him about my piano-playing abilities. He asked if I was interested in auditioning for him for the Wilkinson Brothers' show. I took one quick look around at the screaming kids and countless toys lying around in the aisle and said, *"Definitely!"*

Gary and I, along with Gene, met at the First Baptist Church in Branson. I had sold my keyboard when I first moved to Branson, so I told them I'd buy another one if I got the job. I don't remember what I played, but Gary and Gene were impressed and hired me on the spot. I was now officially back in show business.

While working with the Wilkinson Brothers I got an interesting offer to audition with Mickey Gilley. At this time, Mickey was still traveling the road circuit and making the occasional stops in Branson. I drove over for my audition to the theater where he was performing. As I pulled up in the parking lot, I noticed his tour bus. What I saw scared me to death. On the front of his bus were three words, "Hide Your Daughters." I kept right on driving and never made it to the audition.

I took a part-time job playing piano with the Noblemen instead. The Noblemen were also three brothers who sang together in the afternoons at the Cristy Lane Theater in Branson. Their show schedule worked well with my Wilkinson Brothers' show schedule. I was in heaven!

I had now had two music jobs. Then Cristy's husband, Lee Stoller, came to me and offered me a job playing for Cristy's evening show. Of course, I couldn't leave the Wilkinson Brothers, so I declined the offer. Lee then promptly fired me from the Noblemen's show. He could do that since it was his wife's theater.

My time at the Wilkinson Brothers' show didn't last very long either because the man who owned that theater decided he wasn't making enough money, so he closed up shop. This sent me scrambling for work. You gotta love show business!

For a short period, I worked at the local Branson newspaper handling subscriptions. I didn't mind this job but I loved being in the music business. Their hours are a lot better. Sleep late, go to work for two hours playing music, go home, go work another two hours, go back home and in the process, make really good money. By this point in my life, I was extremely grateful that my mother had bought that $25 piano!

By 1990, I was auditioning for a show at the Roy Clark Celebrity Theater. Roy Clark had lent his name (for some large amount of money) to this theater in Branson. This theater brought in nationally known country music artists for three days at a time, two shows a day.

Gary Wilkinson and I auditioned together and landed this great gig. Our job was to do a one-hour opening act and then the star would come on. I met so many wonderful stars while there. I literally was a part of the opening act for stars like Roy Clark,

Ray Stevens, Loretta Lynn, Conway Twitty, Tammy Wynette, Jim Stafford, Roger Miller, B.J. Thomas and many more.

One of my favorite people was Ricky Skaggs. Ricky is a very quiet man offstage but I got the opportunity to chat with him one afternoon before he went on. We talked about God and the current movie of the time, "Out On A Limb" with Shirley McLaine.

I told him about a book I had just finished reading concerning that particular subject and asked him if he'd like to read it. He surprisingly said yes. I ran home between shows and found the book and brought it back for him. That night as he was getting ready to walk on stage, I caught him and thanked him for being so nice and explained to him that I couldn't stay for his last performance. He held up his show long enough to run back out to his bus and find a couple of books he thought I'd like to read. I've never forgotten his kindness.

By this point, my career was going really well, but my home life was suffering. Patty and I were on two different schedules. She worked early and I worked late. My dream wasn't working out so perfectly. Things got worse as my career continued to soar.

I left the Roy Clark Celebrity Theater at the end of the season to take a job at Silver Dollar City playing for the Branson Brothers. This was also a great gig. The Branson Brothers were an up-and-coming country quartet who performed the night show in the 4,000-seat Echo Hollow Amphitheater there at the park. This place was packed seven nights a week. I played the piano and the accordion in this show.

Working at a theme park has its advantages too. I was able to pick up additional work playing during the day with a western swing band. I'd work five days a week with them and seven nights a week with the Branson Brothers.

During Branson's off-season, I'd hit the road doing dates with the Branson Brothers. They were busy promoting their new record deal with Warner Brothers Records. I learned to love the road. The road is a great place to hide from what's really going on back at home.

While working with the Branson Brothers, I became very good friends with their lead singer, Terry Kaufman. Terry was the most laid-back guy I have ever met. It's a good thing that Terry was a great singer because he would have never kept a real job. The reason being, Terry hated clocks. It was only by the grace of God that he made it to the shows on time. Terry loved everybody. You felt like a million bucks hanging around him.

He and I discovered that we shared a love for gospel music. One particular Easter weekend, we were out traveling on the road with the Branson Brothers and Terry and I had driven together in a car instead of riding the bus because we both had to be back to sing at Easter sunrise services. This one road trip set into motion a dream that would later become a reality.

Terry shared with me how he had wanted the Branson Brothers to pursue a career in gospel music instead of country. I told him of watching the Blackwood Brothers as a kid and my dream to sing in a group. I suggested to him that we should start a part-time gospel group. He loved the idea and the whole way back home we planned how to start it.

Terry was a lead singer and I was a baritone singer. This meant that we needed a tenor singer to have a group. I didn't have to look far to find one either. I called up my best friend, Ashley Ellison, and asked him if he was interested. He jumped at the chance. The three of us got together and there was magic from the very beginning... Terry was the magic! Up to this point, Ashley and I neither one had sung much professionally. Terry taught us so much about singing gospel music and we were both quick learners. We began to sing anywhere we could, mostly Sunday mornings because of our schedules. We called everyone we knew looking for places to sing. Now, we needed a name.

Coming up with a name for any group is hard, but especially for a gospel group because all of the good names are already taken. I knew one thing for certain; I didn't want the word "brothers" in it. I mean after all, I loved the Statler Brothers and the Blackwood Brothers, and I had played for the Wilkinson Brothers and now the Branson Brothers, so anything "brothers" was out!

I honestly can't remember any of the choices we didn't pick, but the name we did agree on, we loved. Matthew 22:14: *"Many are called, but few are chosen."* Thus, the name "Chosen Few" was selected. We quickly went into the recording studio and recorded our first cassette, titled "Steppin' On The Clouds," and we were doing just that.

During this period, I briefly played piano for the Blackwood Quartet, not to be confused with the Blackwood Brothers quartet.

Ron Blackwood was the son of R.W. Blackwood—an original member of the Blackwood Brothers—and the owner of this group. Ron however had just been released from federal prison and was still widely considered the black sheep of that family. I really knew nothing about Ron personally; I was just familiar with his famous last name.

The allure of playing for the Blackwood Quartet quickly faded when I was asked to sing Ron's part from the piano while he stood out front lip-syncing. During one performance, one of the other members of the group introduced Ron as this fantastic singer, to which I rolled my eyes and smiled. I thought that no one had seen me, but his wife did. I was fired right after the show.

Meanwhile, back to Chosen Few. Ashley's mother was still attending church at the same church where I'd met Sue. Sue's father was no longer the pastor there, so Ashley got us scheduled there to sing. To say that I was nervous and anxious about returning to that church would be an understatement. I was downright scared to death. This church held so many memories of my time with Sue. She and her family had lived in the parsonage right next door to the church. Almost everything that Sue and I had experienced, happened right there at that church.

Old feelings and memories began to creep back into my thoughts the closer the date got. That deep, dark secret was getting harder to contain. I know Patty must have noticed changes in my behavior the closer it got to the date of our singing there. I was determined though, to keep it hidden. Then life happened. What I'm getting ready to tell you still amazes even me.

On Saturday night, the night before my scheduled return to Sue's old church, I was at Silver Dollar City playing piano for the Branson Brothers. It was like any other night. The amphitheater was packed with screaming fans and the "brothers" were knocking them dead. Our show was divided into two halves. The first half was about an hour long. Then we'd take a fifteen minute intermission so the "brothers" could sell a gazillion cassette twin packs.

It was customary for the entire cast to make an appearance out front of the stage to greet guests for at least five to seven minutes before returning backstage to prepare for the second half. I went out front just like always, never knowing who I might meet.

Standing there to greet me, the night before my "big return," was Sue's older sister.

Now keep in mind, she knows nothing about my deep, dark secret. To her, I'm just her sister's ex-fiancé and she's excited to see me again. She gives me a big hug and asks me how I'm doing. I give her the standard answer: *"I'm great!"*

She then proceeded to tell me that Sue was back in town and going through a very ugly divorce. She explained that Joe had been physically abusive to her and...are you ready for this... abusive to the *twin boys*! She has no earthly idea what she had just said to me. I politely excused myself and headed backstage... and cried.

What are the odds of this happening? The night before I'm to return to Sue's old church to sing, her sister shows up at my place of work and informs me that I have not just one son, but two... and they along with Sue have been abused. And the icing on the cake...they're back! Five years of guilt and shame poured out of me that night backstage. I don't remember the rest of that show because I went into autopilot.

The next day, I got up early and called information and found Sue's number. I called and explained that I had seen her sister the night before and that I was going to be in the area. She agreed that I could drop by and see her. I have no idea what songs Chosen Few sang that day or how I made it through emotionally. I had one goal...I had to see Sue and the twins for myself. My deep, dark secret was quickly coming unraveled.

I'm writing this as candidly as I can hoping that someone reading this will see from my example that you cannot get ahead of God, and you cannot live your life hiding the truth of your past mistakes, especially from those you love. The price that Patty was to pay in the days ahead was unforgivable. I should have been honest from the start.

My friend, don't ever think that you are smarter than everyone else and that you won't get caught. As you'll see, I was only just beginning to pay for my sins. Luke 8:17 says: *"For there is nothing hidden that will not be disclosed, and nothing concealed that will not be known or brought out into the open."*

If I had done the right thing from the beginning, no one would have been hurt, but sin breeds more sin. If you have un-confessed sin in your life, do the right thing today and go to God and confess it, then go to that friend or that loved one and do the same. Yes it's hard, but you're saving yourself untold future problems.

"It wasn't me who said this man is guilty

And I didn't shout out "Crucify"

I didn't mock His name or point the blame

And say that He should die...

But it was me who held Him to the cross."

–Brian Arnold
(From the song "It Was Me")

Brian's Road Manager, Dan Lyming and Kelsey at TCT

Ashley, Casey, Brian and Scott Chosen Few

Chosen Few onstage at the Andy Williams Moon River Theater in Branson, Missouri

"The man who walks with God always gets to his destination."

—Henrietta Mears

"Delight thyself also in the Lord; and He shall give thee the desires of thine heart."

Psalm 37:4 (KJV)

Chapter Ten

The Beginning Of A Dream

That next morning couldn't come quick enough for me. I'm not really sure that I even slept much that night. I was consumed with thoughts of seeing Sue again and meeting my boys for the first time. I waited until Patty left that morning before making contact.

As I called information to get her number, my heart raced. When the operator came on and gave me the number, I was sweating. What would she say? It had been over five years.

To be honest with you, I don't remember much of our conversation. All I know for sure was the result: I could come and see her at her apartment later that night. She gave me the directions.

Downtown Springfield. North on Campbell. West on Sunshine. North on Fort Street. Apartments on the left with the playground and swing set. Now there was only one problem, I had several hours to wait and a concert to perform at her dad's old church. That day was one of the longest days I've ever experienced.

When I arrived at the church to meet Ashley and Terry, I was nervous. Floods of memories came rushing into my mind. Some of my thoughts were happy, some were sad, but most were feelings of guilt. What could I have done differently? Why hadn't I stood up and done the right thing? I shouldn't be singing today and especially here!

The concert is just a blur in my memory. I don't remember anything about it except that I couldn't wait for it to be over. All I wanted to do was sit down with Sue and figure this all out. I know Ashley and Terry must have thought that I was acting very strange that day. After it was over, I got in my car and headed straight to Sue's apartment.

My mind was racing with all kinds of questions. What would Sue's reaction be to seeing me again after all these years? Did she regret her choices as much as I regretted mine? What would the boys think? Would they like me or accept me?

The biggest mistake I made on this day was not consulting the Lord. I blindly and foolishly made my way to Sue's apartment. I didn't tell my wife, my parents or any of my friends what I was doing. I never thought through any of the consequences of my actions, I had only one driving thought: I must talk to Sue and see my boys. That was it.

When I arrived at her apartment I was like a school kid on his first date. My hands were sweaty and my heart was about to beat right out of my chest. I checked my hair and my teeth in the rearview mirror to make sure I looked presentable, then I headed for the door. I was nervous.

I stood in front of her door for a moment, afraid to ring the bell. All of my self-worth was still tied to this girl. If she rejected me, I was worthless. With all of my being, I wanted her to open that door and take me in her arms and tell me what a terrible mistake she had made in choosing Joe. I reached out and pushed the doorbell, Sue opened the door…and my Hallmark movie of the week reunion didn't take place.

Awkward would probably be the best word to describe our first meeting in five years. There were no hugs or big bright smiles to greet me, only a distant look in her eyes. She invited me in but there were no boys anywhere in sight. I sat down on the couch and looked at her trying to find any kind of connection.

Conversation was difficult to say the least. We made small talk for a while and then I finally mustered up the nerve to ask about the boys. She told me that Austin and Justin were fine and they, along with their younger sister, were upstairs asleep. *Asleep! How could she have put them to sleep when she knew I was coming over!*

I asked if I could see a picture of them, so she found one for me. The picture took my breath away. They looked identical to me! I remember making a remark to that fact but she acted as if she didn't understand why I said that. I looked at her straight in the eyes and asked, *"Don't you remember, Sue?"*

I went on to remind her of everything that had happened five years ago and finally she asked me not to say anything out of fear of what Joe might do. By this point, my heart was completely trampled all over the floor. I didn't care what Joe might do or say, all I wanted to do was make things right.

Sue went on to share horrific things that she and the boys had endured at the hands of Joe, and she convinced me to remain silent and not seek out any legal action against him. I left and walked out of her door that night feeling crushed and defeated. How can you feel sorry for someone, yet mad at him or her at the same time?

Once I was back at home, the guilt returned. I had to tell someone the truth before I went crazy. In hindsight, I should have told Patty first, but instead I called my father and asked to see him. I drove down the next day and informed him that he had two grandsons. His response was not what I wanted or expected.

After a myriad of questions and stern looks, his advice was to leave well enough alone, but that wasn't the response I was looking for. I went back even more confused about what to do. I eventually told Patty and she reacted as most women probably would have…she was upset. She couldn't understand why I had hidden this from her and she was also upset that she wouldn't be the one to give me my first child. This became a wedge between us and I know that I didn't handle things correctly.

Meanwhile, Chosen Few continued to sing. Ashley and I started taking it more seriously than Terry. We wanted to go full-time, but Terry was already singing full-time, now with the Blackwood Quartet.

While working with the Blackwood Quartet, I had met a young man from Milan, Tennessee, named David Fountain. David was a very charismatic individual who loved Southern Gospel music, especially quartet music. He and I became friends because of our love of the

Cathedral Quartet, and he began to travel with us to our church dates for moral support.

Terry, being the free spirit that he was, could never be depended on to show up for our concerts and David was eager, willing and able to fill in at the last minute. David knew almost every gospel song by heart and on top of that, he was a great emcee. David could talk an Eskimo into buying air conditioning for his igloo! David also had quite a testimony. We would even bring him up out of the audience just to share how he had overcome cancer. David moved people. As Terry became less and less reliable, we depended on David more and more.

By the winter of 1992, I had gotten the news that Silver Dollar City was going to hire a new, resident southern Gospel quartet. Ashley and I immediately began to put together a plan to try out for the position.

We had only three major problems. One, Ashley would have to give up his full-time job with benefits at Kraft Foods. Of course, he was more than willing to do that. Two, Terry wasn't interested in starting all over with a brand new group, so Ashley and I asked David if he were interested in joining Chosen Few. Of course, he was also more than willing. The third major problem was we were a trio, not a quartet. In order for us to be considered for the job we had to have a bass singer.

Earlier that summer, we had done a few fill-in dates at Silver Dollar City with Terry's friend, bass singer, Ray Burdett. Ray had performed on Hee-Haw with the Hee-Haw Gospel Quartet and was a fantastic singer, but he also wasn't interested in starting all over.

Finding a bass singer became our number-one priority. David and I had met a young man from Asheville, North Carolina by the name of Jody Medford while working with the Blackwood Quartet.

Jody was a great bass singer with a fantastic smile but he lived several states away from Missouri. To our surprise, Jody was looking for a change in his life so he agreed to come out for a visit and see if we could get the job. We spent a couple of days rehearsing in my living room, culminating with a concert at the First Baptist Church in Branson. Now, it was off to audition at Silver Dollar City.

We were greenhorns for sure. Jody had the most quartet experience of the four of us because he had sung with Squire Parsons and with the Anchormen before joining Chosen Few. The rest of us had only sung in part-time groups, but we were determined to get this job. We were hungry for it.

The audition took place during Silver Dollar City's Christmas festival, outside at the old Gazebo stage. The reason I point this out is because it was wintertime and it was cold. It was so cold that I had to put a heat lamp next to my keyboard in order to keep my hands warm while I played.

We had a thirty-minute set to perform for our audition. It was good that it was only thirty minutes because that was all the songs we had time to learn. There was a small crowd present while we sang and we gave them our all. We sang "Just A Little Talk With Jesus" so that we could feature how good Jody was at singing bass, and "I'll Fly Away" so that I could pound the piano in that Southern Gospel style. Ashley sang like a woman, like tenor singers are supposed to, and David talked his way into their hearts. It must have worked because after our set, we were hired on the spot. Chosen Few was now officially a full-time Gospel quartet.

Silver Dollar City's next season didn't start until April of 1993, so that meant that we had three months to hit the road and sing in churches to help prepare us for what lay ahead. It also meant that we had three months to record two cassette projects worth of Gospel music so that we would have product to sell. We immediately began calling every relative, friend and friends of friends begging for churches to let us come and sing. We were literally nobodies and it was only by the grace of God that we were able to survive those three months financially.

Probably the biggest help in getting us in the studio and on the road was Jim and Anne Newton from St. Louis. I had met Jim and Anne while working with the Branson Brothers at Silver Dollar City. They took regular visits to Branson and actually were good friends with Terry when I met them. Jim and Anne took a chance on four boys with very limited experience and loaned us enough money to record, buy a small sound system, and to buy a conversion van that we affectionately called the "Vus."

The reason we called it this was because the "Vus" was bigger than a van but smaller than a bus. Later, we added a trailer to pull behind it and we felt like we were traveling in style. We owe so much to Jim and Anne. The greatest gift they gave us though was their love and friendship.

In between traveling on weekends and singing in churches, we now found ourselves in a recording studio feverishly working to get some product ready. A big part of a group's income is their product sales and we were in desperate need to get something done—and quick. I called on my friend Jamie Haage to help us.

Jamie and I had worked together as part of the Branson Brothers band at Silver Dollar City. He played almost every instrument and he had just opened his own recording studio outside of Branson. Our first two cassette projects were the number six and seven projects ever recorded in his studio.

The studio quickly became my home away from home. It provided a nice escape from my problems. Since I had the most musical experience of the four of us in Chosen Few, I was in charge of producing the projects. Almost all of the songs were selected and arranged by me, and I even wrote a couple of the songs.

One of the songs I wrote was "Miracles," and it became the title song to the first cassette project. I had actually written this song as a senior in high school during my senior English class, not because it was an assignment but because I was bored. This song quickly became an audience favorite. Even though the lyrics are pretty elementary, the thought is genuine.

My love of the Statler Brothers' music was evident with us recording "He Is There," "Jesus Is The Answer Every Time," and "Noah Found Grace In The Eyes Of The Lord," with the first two being Statler originals.

Another song I chose for our first project was a Mike Adkins original, "Do You Know What I Just Did Mister?" This song quickly became one of our most requested songs. I had originally heard it on Mike's solo record as a child and my mother insisted that I learn it to sing as a special for church.

I didn't have the music in written form so I learned it by ear. It was a song about a man seeing a little boy on the steps of a building on his way to church and inviting him in for the service. The little boy hears what the preacher says about needing to be saved and turns to the man who invited him saying, *"Do you know what I just did Mister? I asked Jesus inside. 'Cause He's standing at my heart's door knocking, I asked Him in for the rest of my life."*

The song and its narrative had made such an impression on me that I felt it would make an excellent Chosen Few song. I slowed the tempo down quite a bit from the original and Jamie added violin and his own unique background vocals to the track. The result was an instant Chosen Few classic. I would eventually record it again for my solo CD, "This Close To Home."

Once while singing in Collinsville, Illinois, I got to hear the real story behind the song. After our concert was over the pastor came and explained that he had to head on home to his wife that was sick, so he purchased some CDs and left. We continued tearing down our sound equipment and about twenty minutes later the pastor returned to the church. He found me and began to tell me that on his way home, while going through the drive-thru at McDonald's, he heard the song "Do You Know What I Just Did Mister?" on the CD he had just purchased.

He had come back to inform us that the song was based on a true story and that he was the preacher talked about in the song! A powerful song became even more powerful to us that night.

The second cassette project Chosen Few recorded was one of traditional church songs that we titled, "The Classics." This included such favorites as "Amazing Grace," "I'll Fly Away," and "How Great Thou Art."

That wonderful song, "How Great Thou Art," would prove to be the standard that we sang in every concert. Of all of the songs

Chosen Few recorded, this song was the most requested of them all. Throughout the process of recording these two projects, Jamie and I became very close friends. Today, Jamie is a successful studio owner, singer, songwriter, musician and one of Branson's most celebrated comedians. I'm blessed to call him my friend.

The dream that had begun as a child listening to the Statler Brothers, and then seeing the Blackwood Brothers in concert, was finally becoming a reality. For the first time in my life I began to realize the gift that God had given me. I had grown up under the shadow of my artificial leg, but now I could see the light bulb shining brightly above my head.

What the enemy meant to harm me at the age of six, God turned around and caused to be a blessing. Romans 8:28 says: "And we know that all things work together for good to them that love God, to them who are called according to His purpose." The devil wants you and I to believe that we have no hope, but with God there is ALWAYS hope. We have to learn to wait upon the Lord.

God is not a short-order cook desperately waiting to fill your request. You are also not in the drive-thru of McDonald's where you pull up, place your prayer request at the first window, then drive twenty feet to the second window where the result you wanted is waiting. It takes trusting the Lord and waiting on Him, because in His time and in His way, He *will* make your dreams come true.

"You still perform miracles for me

Just look at this life and you can see

To change me from my wicked ways

And point me to the Light

I say, You still perform miracles for me."

–Brian Arnold
(From the song "Miracles")

"Today is your day, your mountain is waiting, so get on your way."

–Dr. Seuss

"Your wound is as deep as the sea. Who can heal you?"

Lamentations 2:13b

Chapter Eleven

Oh, What a Tangled Web We Weave...

As my career and ministry began to take off, my personal life continued to become a tangled mess. Even now as I reflect back on everything that happened, I still hurt for those my actions affected. So often we get tunnel vision when we're going through the valleys of life and lose sight of the bigger picture God has for us.

The news that I had twin five-year-old boys began to have a ripple effect in the lives of those closest to me. At the time, I couldn't understand why Patty was so disappointed and hurt by my deep, dark secret. To me, she shouldn't have been anymore offended or surprised as anyone else. I had kept this from everyone, not just her.

We had already been drifting apart because of my new "entertainer" lifestyle and opposite work schedules. All I could see was that she was not being very understanding of the pain that I had been carrying all those years. I never gave any consideration to the hurt this caused her because my expectation was for everyone, including her, to feel sorry for me! So when she began to question my deception, I took it as an attack and ran.

I began to withdraw from anyone who didn't agree with me. If I felt any kind of guilt trip coming on from someone, then I completely disassociated myself from them. I didn't act rationally and I definitely didn't want Godly counsel unless it was from someone who "understood" my plight.

In hindsight, I should have sought out a counselor. I honestly had no idea just how messed up I was psychologically and emotionally. Even though Patty was hurt and angry because of what I had done, God could have restored our relationship had I chosen to let Him. However, I continued to run from confrontation. I felt like I was the only one who was a victim. How dare anyone point a finger at me…

Working with Chosen Few at Silver Dollar City gave me a false sense of justification. *"God must understand and agree with me because look at how He's blessing my career! He wants me to be happy too!!"* Believe me, I wasn't happy. It was time to clean the slate and start over. I rationalized that I never should have married Patty to begin with and that she would never let me live it down that I had deceived her.

I felt that it was totally unfair for her to hold this over my head because all of this happened way before I knew her. The logical choice: start over. Besides, I had met someone at work that I just knew would *really* understand me.

Ah, yes…the ugly truth. I can see it today, but back then it was all clouded in justification and the right to be happy… yada, yada,

yada. Although there was not a physical affair going on, my mind was racing once again with the possibilities of *finally* being truly happy and understood.

Sue didn't want me. Patty was disappointed and angry with me. My life seemed to be an endless trail of pain and heartaches, so I fell back on the only reasonable thing I knew to do: find someone else to love me for who I was. I didn't realize it at the time, but the problem was that I didn't like myself. I was a victim.

One day while Patty was at work, I packed up all my belongings, put them in a storage unit and moved in with Ashley and his wife. I know this was a very cowardly thing to do but I didn't want to fight and I definitely didn't want to see her cry. I didn't want to hear what she had to say, either. I just wanted it all to go away.

I can only imagine how Patty must have felt that day when she came home to find that I had moved out. Even though she tried to get me to reconcile, I wanted nothing of it. I just wanted to move on. I quickly filed for divorce and immediately started my life over with no regard for Patty. I heard that she remarried. Since our divorce, we have not had any contact. I can only hope that she has or will find it in her heart to forgive me. I offer up no defense for my actions. I was wrong and I am truly sorry for hurting her.

The ripple effect I talked about earlier began to move on out. Needless to say, my parents were very disappointed and angry about my decision to end my three-year marriage. I'm sure that no parent wants his child to act so irresponsibly, but the pressure of being a pastor and having a congregation of people watching every move you and your family makes can sometimes seem unbearable.

What I never took into consideration was the pressure my actions put on my dad. I knew that Dad had felt a tremendous amount of pressure because of what happened to me at age six. The weight of what he felt he had done by running over me with a lawnmower, only he knows. He had always felt he was under the gun by somebody.

As a coach, he had the pressure to win or he could potentially lose his job. As a school administrator, he had the pressure of keeping teachers happy, to preparing a budget and staying on that budget, to dealing with unhappy parents who felt their child was being unfairly punished, to then that parent deciding to run for the school board and trying to get him fired. No wonder Dad seldom had a smile on his face at work.

But now, here he was a pastor with the responsibility of "equipping the Saints." People look to him for advice and counsel on how best to handle their problems and then they see his son. *"How can you advise us on how to live if you can't even raise your own son to live right?"* Talk about pressure! Although I'm sure probably no one from his little country church ever said anything like that to him, I know he had to wonder if they were thinking it.

My divorce from Patty immediately put a wedge between my parents and me. Most of it was due to my fear of really dealing with everything that had happened to me. I didn't want to face what I really thought of myself, let alone have more guilt piled on top of me. All I wanted to do was pursue my own ideas of what I thought would make me happy.

After I left Patty, I immediately began pursuing with full court pressure the lady I had met at Silver Dollar City. Her name was

Diane Kukal. She was a very attractive and independent redhead who worked as a floral designer at Mary's Flowers there on the park. Chosen Few performed daily at the Gazebo stage right in the center of the square. This was the hub of activity for Silver Dollar City—the square, not Chosen Few! At some point throughout the day, people who entered the park found themselves on the square. This is where I met Diane.

If you've never been to Silver Dollar City—a 19th century theme park nestled in the Ozark Mountains of southern Missouri—you are seriously missing a treat. In the summer, the sound of June-bugs, the smell of funnel cakes, and the sight of vintage blacksmiths, sheriffs, and ladies twirling pink parasols takes one back to a simpler time. A hotter time, too! It can get pretty hot and humid at "the City" during the peak season, but that doesn't keep record-breaking crowds from crowding in and enjoying the fun.

At first, I would smile at Diane, as she would pass by on her way to the employee lounge. Then I found myself taking trips between shows to the flower shop to see her. Everybody knew I was crazy about Diane, everybody that is except my family, whom I was careful not to mention anything to. I knew they would not approve. How could they? After all, I wasn't even technically divorced yet. I knew that they would assume I had left Patty for greener pastures, so I left well enough alone. Besides, Diane wasn't showing a lot of signs of being interested in me anyway. She wasn't just playing hard to get, she *was* hard to get!

Diane was the single mother of an eight-year-old little girl named Kelsey. Due to some weird circumstances concerning Kelsey's father, (which I'm not going into here), and some bad past relationships, Diane was not looking for a "relationship." This, of course, was exactly was I was looking for. I had no desire to be alone. The only pictures I had of happiness were the ones like I had seen depicted on the movie screens, where two people meet, fall hopelessly in love and live happily ever after. Hollywood has an amazing way of shaping our ideas of what happiness should look like.

Diane had no way to resist me, though! I was everywhere she was. I spent my breaks in her shop and walked her to her car. I followed her to the employee lounge and sat with her for lunch. I wrote songs for her and I even wrote love notes to her and had them delivered by various people who worked at the park with me. I continually asked her out and she continually said no. This did not deter me at all! I was determined to win her affection.

Does this sound remotely familiar to any of my actions of the past at all? Talk about tunnel vision! Even as I think about all of this now, I'm amazed that I couldn't see the flaw in my plan. I *never* consulted the Lord for *any* direction concerning my life. That is not to imply anything negative toward Diane, Sue or Patty, but simply to point out that doing the same thing over and over and expecting different results is the definition of insanity. (Thanks Albert!) My problem was really an identity problem. I didn't know who I was and I thought being in a relationship was the answer. It certainly worked well for Mike and Carol of The Brady Bunch. Why not me?

After countless refusals, Diane finally relented and agreed to go out on a date with me. (I guess I'm good at wearing people down!) Our first couple of dates was simple and involved meeting somewhere, with Kelsey, and then heading home separately. I had no idea the twist that was soon coming my way.

During this time, I had little to no contact with Sue and my boys. She had thoroughly convinced me that Joe was violent and would cause great harm to her and the boys if I stirred up things about the past. I was really at a loss for what to do. Everyone but me seemed content to leave well enough alone. My heart ached to know my sons, and from time to time, even to be with Sue.

The only thing I really knew about my sons were their names. I felt terrible. My sin seemed unforgivable to me. Even though somewhere in my mind I knew God had forgiven me, I still wrestled with it. *Had God really forgiven me? Could Austin and Justin ever forgive me? Would they ever know who I was?*

By this point, I was living in an apartment in Springfield off of Battlefield. I knew Diane lived somewhere in Springfield as well, but I had never been invited over. Then one night after celebrating Kelsey's ninth birthday at a local skating rink, Diane asked me if I would help her by bringing some of the girls from the birthday party back to her apartment because she couldn't fit them all into her car. Of course, I was eager to oblige.

Since I had never been to Diane's apartment, I was following her street by street and turn by turn, so as not to get lost. North on Campbell. West on Sunshine. North on Fort Street...

Fort Street? My mind started racing. *No way! Surely not!* I started sweating and getting a bit nervous. As I pulled into the parking lot of her apartment, I found myself speechless, staring at the same playground and swing set I had looked at almost a year earlier...the night I came to visit Sue. *You have got to be kidding me! What are the odds?* As I got out of my brand new Dodge Dakota pickup, you could have knocked me over with a feather.

Diane noticed the odd look on my face and was immediately concerned that I was somehow offended that she and Kelsey lived in low-income housing. Of course, that was the furthest thing from my mind. I was completely dumbfounded. *Am I on "Candid Camera"?* Or as in today's world, *am I being "Punked"?*

She invited me inside and after the kids were situated, I unloaded my deep, dark secret on her. My cool façade was gone. Diane and Kelsey were neighbors to Sue and my boys! Kelsey actually knew them and had played together with them in the playground. I'm thinking to myself, *"This nine-year-old girl knows Austin and Justin better than I do!"*

From that moment on, Diane and I were in a "relationship." She understood what I had been going through because of the challenges concerning Kelsey's father. Diane was emphatic that I *needed* to be a part of my sons' lives and this was music to my ears, even an answer to my unspoken prayers. Soon after, I moved in with Diane. This was a well-kept secret, especially from my parents, but I felt justified in doing so because this was now all about me being around my sons. I wanted to know more than just their names.

Father's Day was right around the corner from Kelsey's birthday, so Diane rented a video camera and videotaped Kelsey playing in the playground with Austin and Justin. (Yes…there actually was a time when very few people had video recorders and no, we didn't have cell phones with video cameras on them either!)

Watching that video on Father's Day was the very first time I had ever seen my boys, other than the picture Sue had shown me that night in her apartment. Up to that point, I had scarcely given any thought to celebrating my being a father. It had always been cloaked in shame and disappointment. Diane's gift that year was the best Father's Day gift I have ever received.

All in all, 1993 was one of the more interesting years of my life. Even though Sue was definitely not happy that I was living right down from her and the boys, it did provide an incredible opportunity for me to actually get to know Austin and Justin. Talk about surreal! Meeting them for the first time was very emotional for me. They thought they were just meeting a friend of Kelsey's. Mind-boggling, isn't it?

Inevitably, Sue would need a babysitter from time to time and I eventually convinced her that I was the logical choice. Of course, everything always hinged on my promise to never say anything about the "real" truth, and whether or not her current boyfriend of the moment was threatened by my involvement. Even though Austin and Justin loved visiting and occasionally spending the night with us, Sue decided to move on *and* that meant without my involvement.

As hard as this was, I had little to say about the matter. I sought legal counsel, but at that time, in Missouri, the statute of limitations was five years to assert one's right as a father. My hands were tied. They eventually moved out of the apartments and communication was all but stopped.

By this point, Diane and I were making wedding plans and dealing with our own unique blending of families. No, I'm not talking about my parents because they were still in the dark about everything concerning Diane and I. I'm actually referring to Kelsey and me.

Kelsey had spent the first nine years of her life being the center of her mother's attention, and now I was a constant threat to that.

Suddenly, I was a full-time father and I felt completely inadequate. I began to realize what a challenge being a parent really is. Don't get me wrong, Kelsey was a great kid, it was just quite a change for me to go from hiding that I was really a father to *really* being a father. To say the least, it was a learning experience for us both.

By the close of the year, Diane and I, with the help of Kelsey, had bought a house closer to Branson. The drive from Springfield had really begun to get long, and with no real involvement with my boys, it seemed like a good decision. Although we weren't married, I rationalized in my mind that we were engaged.

Winter was fast approaching and Silver Dollar City was closing for the season. This meant that Chosen Few would soon be hitting the road. It also meant that it was time to hire a new bass singer. Jody Medford had been hired away from us by a local music theater, which left us scrambling to replace him. Fortunately, we didn't have to look too far.

Ashley remembered singing with a guy from his college days that had a four-and-a-half-octave range. His name was Scott Fraker. We gave him a call one day and told him we had a position open for a bass singer, and asked him if he would consider auditioning for us. After a little friendly persuasion, he consented.

Scott was an immediate answer to our prayers. Not only could he sing bass incredibly well, but he also had tremendous stage presence. He accepted our offer and gave notice to his employer just as our road season began.

Our first Sunday to sing together was on January 16, 1994, my father's birthday, in Marshfield, Mo. It was a cold, winter morning as I pulled onto I-44. The other guys in my quartet were also in their cars on the interstate, some in front of me and some behind. We were caravanning our way to the church and expectations were high.

All of a sudden my Dodge Dakota pickup hit black ice and began spinning out of control. It all happened so fast. I slid across the median into oncoming traffic and ended up broadside in the road, drifting backwards. I watched as a semi-truck loaded with steel beams jack-knifed, trying to avoid hitting me, but to no avail. He crashed into the side of my pickup, knocking the bed of my truck completely off.

The force of the impact jerked my vehicle around, causing me to be hit again by the semi. The left side of my neck took the brunt of the crash as the seatbelt kept my body from being hurled out through the window.

The big truck flipped over in the middle of the interstate, spilling steel beams everywhere. The driver's side door of my pickup was sprung open and I found myself hanging by my neck out the door in the seatbelt, wide-awake. My keyboard, which had been over on the passenger's side of my truck, was now resting behind my back, almost as if trying to help hold me up. I was unable to do anything but hang there. One thing I definitely noticed, I couldn't move my left arm at all.

The wormhole was now closing and reality was coming back into full view.

"Now this is not the end. It is not even the beginning of the end. But it is, perhaps, the end of the beginning."

—Winston Churchill

My grace is sufficient for you, for my power is made perfect in weakness.

2 Corinthians 12:9

Chapter Twelve

Hanging On By a Thread

S cott was the first one to get to me. He had been driving right behind me when I started to lose control. A helpless feeling came over him as he watched the semi-truck hit me and flip over. He immediately pulled his car over to the side of the road and instinctively jumped out. For a moment, he almost forgot that a car on the interstate could hit him, too.

Scott tried as quickly as he could to get to me, which was no easy task. He was wearing dress shoes and keeping his footing was a bit of a problem since ice was beginning to form everywhere on the ground. A million thoughts were running through his mind as he approached my truck. Everything from *"Is he alive?"* to, *"This is a great way to start my new job!"*

As he came around to the driver's side of my pickup, he saw that the door was open and that I was suspended in the seatbelt. My legs were hanging almost in a kneeling position under the truck, yet my knees could not quite reach the ground. My artificial leg had come off and was lying in the middle of the road amidst the debris. He also noticed several lacerations on my face from where the broken glass had cut me.

Scott quickly grabbed hold of me and began trying to support the weight of my body and take the strain of the seatbelt off my neck. Although I was awake, I wasn't any help. As Scott struggled to keep his shoes from slipping and trying to lift me up, a man from out of nowhere showed up and began to help him. The man just happened to have a pocketknife and a blanket. Together, he and Scott cut me out of the seatbelt, and placing me face first on the ground, they covered me up with the blanket and Scott's overcoat.

Snow Angel

I drive by the wreck site every day; live right by it.

That morning, we were four vehicles, all in a line going to a church concert. Brian was in the lead vehicle.

Just past Stafford, I looked in my rear-view mirror; a split-second later, I turned my attention back to the scene in front of me. In a truly surreal moment, I saw a semi sliding down the interstate! Next thought: *where is Brian?*

I hadn't seen Brian go into median. I saw the vehicles colliding, literally as it happened.

In such a moment, the mind focuses on one quick scene after another, a series of freeze-frames.

First, the trailer carrying steel girders...they were being scattered *everywhere*. Then I stopped and realized, there's black ice. I concentrated on getting to the side of the road, to get my vehicle stopped. Stuff was everywhere!

I then realized Brian was across the median, across the interstate. His driver's side door was open. Brian was out of the door, suspended by his shoulder belt. In a scene straight out of an independent film, his prosthetic leg was back up the interstate! His other leg was hanging completely out the door.

I took off running and when I got to him, he was held in place by the shoulder strap. Brian was conscious, but couldn't move. Try as I might, I couldn't move him off that strap. I noticed he had swelling around the neck (we'd later find out this was a grisly condition known as "hangman's fracture.")

Here's where this part of the story really begins.

A gentleman came up to me. I was also aware that our quartet mate, Ashley, had seen everything unfold and was on his way back.

The man came up to me. I was trying frantically to get Brian out of the belt. The man said he had a knife, and so he cut the seatbelt off. We lay Brian down in the snow, and I took off my trenchcoat. This helpful man had a blanket and put it on him.

Keep in mind, it's all happening so fast. The collision. Racing toward Brian. Assessing the situation on the fly. Then this Samaritan in the nick of time.

Added to the mix was the fact that by the time the first responder arrived, another car had been involved in a wreck. The icy conditions were indeed treacherous.

I asked first responder where the guy was that helped and he said, "What guy?"

As the responders were stabilizing Brian, I stood up and looked up and down the snowy strip of road.

The sleet was now coming down hard. I peered into the distance.

No one was there; not the man or his vehicle. I have decided that I won't know who he is until I get to heaven.

–Scott Fraker

While all of this was going on, Ashley and his wife, Michelle, had turned around and had located an emergency phone alongside the highway. The call was made and help was on the way. In no time at all, a first responder made it to the scene.

As the first responder knelt down to begin checking on me, the sound of another crash rang out. He and Scott looked up to see that a car had just crashed into the first responder's vehicle. All they could do was shrug their shoulders.

Scott then noticed that his helper with the pocketknife and blanket was nowhere to be found. He asked the first responder if he had seen where the man had gone. His response was, *"What other man? You're the only one that I've seen."* I personally do not remember anything about this mystery man, but to this day, Scott believes that he was an angel. I know Scott to be a good, honest man, who would not make something like this up. It is a comforting thought to know that angels really are watching over us.

By this time, Ashley had made his way to where I was and had gotten down on his knees beside me. He did his best to encourage me but I knew that this was serious. I kept saying, *"I can't move my left arm at all."* Ice continued to build up as it fell from the heavens. There would be no air-evac helicopter coming for me in this weather.

Finally, after what seemed to be an eternity, an ambulance arrived. Two EMTs jumped out and quickly moved into action. The first EMT came over to where I was and began accessing my injuries the best he could. The other EMT went to check on the semi-truck driver. After concluding that he was ok, he looked around to see if there was anyone else in need of medical attention.

It was at this point that the EMT, a medical professional, noticed my artificial leg in the middle of the highway. The problem was, he didn't realize that it's fake and started exclaiming, *"He's lost a leg too!"* I'm lying face-down alongside the highway, scared, with my arm not moving, and I start laughing. I'm thinking to myself, *"If this is the help they've sent me...I'm going to die!"* What I didn't know at the time was that my life was really hanging on by a thread.

Eventually, I was carefully put onto a stretcher and placed into the ambulance. The guys followed behind as we slowly made our way to the emergency room of St. John's Hospital in Springfield. Once there, doctors and nurses swarmed into a flurry of activity. It was obvious that my injuries were life-threatening.

Their first concern was not my arm but the swelling around my neck where the shoulder strap of my seatbelt had absorbed most of the impact of the wreck. The swelling was beginning to constrict the flow of air through my windpipe. I can still remember the ER doctor saying that if they couldn't place a breathing tube down my throat, they would have to do a tracheotomy. I definitely did NOT want them to do that. Memories of my Uncle Gene and his tracheotomy flashed through my mind. Calming myself as much as I could, I relaxed my throat and allowed the breathing tube to be slid into place. Once my breathing could be regulated, I finally passed out.

Somewhere along the way, a couple phone calls were made, by Ashley and his wife, Michelle. One was to Diane. Not wanting to scare her too much and realizing her deathly fear of driving in wintry conditions, Michelle explained that I had been in an accident but that they didn't think it was too serious. They told her that I was being taken to the hospital to be checked out and that they would keep her informed once they knew more details.

At first, Diane tried to go back to sleep but a nagging feeling in the pit of her stomach told her she needed to call her brother, Gary, who lived in Springfield. She told him about the accident and asked him if he would go over to the hospital and check in on me since she hated driving with ice on the roads. Gary willingly agreed to go, so he and his wife, Deb, headed over to St. John's.

Another call was made to my sister, Shelley, who also lived in Springfield. Shelley had recently been battling Hodgkin's Disease. I had not had much contact with any of my family since my divorce from Patty, and not being there for her in her time of struggle had been tough on our relationship. But in times of tragedy, personal things must be put aside, and that's exactly what Shelley did. She immediately called my mom and dad and informed them about my accident. She then headed for the hospital.

The news hit my dad especially hard. Although our relationship was strained, I was still his son. I'm sure all kinds of thoughts were running through his mind, and on top of everything else, January 16th is his birthday. Some kind of birthday present, huh?

A Father Remembers

Our first reaction to the phone call that Brian had been in a terrible wreck and was in intensive care was one of shock, not another accident. It was a long ride to Springfield that icy day. When we went into the intensive care to see him, it was a devastating experience for both of us. Again, we knew it was a life-changing experience. I remember thinking, how will he survive this emotionally, let alone physically? He faced it with incredible strength and determination. Like his grandfather, he never let his handicap slow him down.

Most of the thoughts and anguish came later with each passing day. I get emotional every time I see him perform because I see a man with one leg and a paralyzed arm who never let life defeat him. He could have sat down and drawn disability, but that was not his character. Through it all, he is a witness for Christ with his music and preaching of God's Word. What more could a mother and father hope for?

–Bob Arnold

Diane's brother, Gary, (whose birthday is also January 16th), got to the hospital and was brought up to speed by Ashley. After realizing the seriousness of my condition, he called Diane and told her that she HAD to find a way to the hospital because they didn't expect me to live.

The news that my accident was life-threatening hit Diane and Kelsey like a ton of bricks. They were overwhelmed with a sense of urgency to get to the hospital but Diane knew there was no way she could drive in such a winter storm. She began to call anyone and everyone looking for help and prayers for me.

One call she made was to her boss at Silver Dollar City, Candy Owen. Candy immediately made a few calls, and after some gentle pleading, was successful in lining up two men with a four-wheel-drive pickup to come and take Diane and Kelsey to the hospital.

Diane didn't know the men and can't remember their names, just that they were willing to help.

There was still one other problem to overcome before Diane and Kelsey could head toward Springfield. There was no way, even with a four-wheel-drive pickup, that anyone could get to our home because we live on the side of a steep hill. Diane was going to have to walk in snow and ice, and in freezing temperatures, over a quarter of a mile—all up hill, with her nine-year-old daughter and their overnight bag to meet the two men.

Both of them were determined that they had to get to the hospital as quickly as possible, so out into the elements they went, struggling against Mother Nature, to meet up with the two men coming to their rescue. Once safely in the pickup, they began the long, slow journey to Springfield, never getting over 25 mph. What normally would have been a forty-five minute trip, took well over two hours.

The first person Kelsey remembers meeting at the hospital was Pastor Larry Hintz of Trinity Lutheran Church, Gary's home church. Pastor Hintz gave her a big hug as she began to cry in his arms. Diane immediately located her brother to get the latest update on me. Gary began to explain that they were concerned about internal injuries, especially a blood clot that could potentially go to my brain and kill me.

I had been in and out of consciousness quite a bit, but every time I came to, I asked for Diane. I was so scared and needed to see a friendly, loving face. I had no idea just how serious my condition really was, but I could tell by the look on everyone's face that it must be grim. I still couldn't move my left arm at all. I needed to see Diane and have her reassure me that everything would be all right.

The doctors were a bit reluctant to let Diane in to see me at first since she was technically not family, but because I was repeatedly asking for her, they relented. Kelsey, of course, also wanted to go in and see me. Eventually the doctors agreed to let them both in, mainly because they didn't expect me to live.

Once inside the intensive care unit, the sight of me was quite gruesome. I had tubes coming out of me everywhere. My eye was swollen, my neck was enlarged, and I had cuts on my face. As soon as I saw them, I began to cry. I couldn't speak because of the breathing tube, so I began to spell out words by writing letters with my finger into Diane's hand. The first thing I wrote was "*Please don't leave me!*"

As tough as all this was to comprehend and deal with, there was still more. My parents were already in the waiting room trying to figure out how to handle what had just happened to their son, when in walks their my fiancé, who by the way, he lives with in a home they've bought together, AND she has a nine-year-old daughter. Not exactly how I planned for them to find all this out!

Awkward is not an adequate word for what was unfolding in that waiting room. No one really knew what to say or even how to react. My world was crashing in all around me, but I was the fortunate one because I didn't have to sit in that waiting room. Even with all these difficulties, everyone pulled together and focused on the main problem at hand…me! (Joke intended.)

According to the doctors there wasn't much hope for me to live. The main concern was a vertebral artery dissection, which is a tear of the inner lining of the vertebral artery. This artery is located in the neck and supplies blood to the brain. The thought was that a blood clot would eventually form, dislodge, and go to my brain and kill me. It would later be determined that this caused me to have a light stroke. Also at this point, I had a hematoma the size of a football on my neck. A hematoma is a localized collection of blood, usually in liquid form within the tissue.

Basically, it became a waiting game. Even though things were a bit precarious between my family and Diane, differences were put aside, even if only temporarily. At one point, Diane and Dad were both in the intensive care unit with me when Diane noticed that one of my pupils was larger than the other. She whispered to my dad to see if he had also noticed it.

He leaned over me to take a quick look and agreed that one was indeed larger than the other. When they asked one of the medical staff about it, they examined me and immediately rushed Diane and Dad out of the room.

Apparently, this was a sign of even more problems. I was taken for more tests and the results showed that I had a C2-3 neck fracture. This also could have been life-threatening had it continued to go undetected. The doctors later agreed that my hematoma had actually been a godsend because it had helped stabilize my neck.

One thing is for sure, a "waiting room" is the appropriate name given to the room where the only thing you can do is wait. Hour after long hour, my friends and family did just that...wait. The doctors had finally said, *"We've done all we can do. It's in God's hands now."*

For almost three days, all anyone could do was wait and pray, and pray they did. People from everywhere began to call upon the Lord that He would spare my life. Diane was giving daily updates to the local gospel radio station, KWFC. Gary Longstaff and Dave Taylor were faithful to inform their 100,000-watt listening audience of my progress and remind everyone to keep me in their prayers.

With each passing day, I got a little bit stronger. Although I was still in critical condition, by the following Wednesday all of the tubes were taken out of me and I was breathing on my own.

Unknown to me, Diane and my folks had finally received some news on my paralyzed left arm. Dr. Mark Crabtree began to explain to them that I had suffered a brachial plexus stretch injury. The brachial plexus is a network of nerves that conducts signals from the spinal cord to the shoulder, arm and hand.

Although the nerves were not completely torn away from the spinal cord, Dr. Crabtree said there was a distinct possibility that they were permanently damaged. The decision was made not to tell me any of this because at this point, who wants to tell someone, especially a piano player, that his or her arm may never work again.

As if I needed anything else to deal with, there was another problem looming. I didn't have any medical insurance. Chosen Few originally had a group medical policy, but due to a disagreement with the company over its lack of payment on a maternity claim, the policy had been dropped. Being four young, healthy guys, we figured that there wasn't a rush on getting another policy in place. Needless to say, we were wrong.

With each passing day, the bills began to mount and fear began to grow. *What am I going to do?* I mean after all, I had a new house to pay for and the medical bills were stacking up. It was obvious that I wasn't going on tour with Chosen Few anytime soon. *What will happen to Chosen Few?*

Ashley, Scott and David definitely had some serious problems to deal with. Not only were they a man short, but they were also now without a piano player. They had concert dates scheduled and their income depended on them continuing on. After a quick meeting, it was decided that Terry Kaufman, the original lead singer of the trio Chosen Few, would be the most logical choice to step in and sing.

Since it was the off-season for Branson, Terry was available and was more than willing to help the guys out. However, they still needed a piano player. They didn't have to look very far. David's wife, Lori, was an accomplished pianist and she too, was more than eager to pitch in and help.

As hard as it must have been, the guys didn't skip a beat. They continued traveling and doing concerts, and when they weren't on the road, they took turns coming to the hospital to check on me. Scott calls it a real faith-building time. Even though things were difficult and money was tight, the guys never once failed to give me a paycheck every week. God truly provided and made a way where there seemed to be no way. I'll never be able to adequately thank the guys of Chosen Few for their generosity and faithfulness to me in my time of need.

Many other people reached out to me as well, either by visiting or with gifts of flowers and cards with money in them. Silver Dollar City, along with my buddies, the Branson Brothers, began to plan a benefit concert at the Grand Palace in Branson. I was definitely lucky to be alive but even more blessed to have such wonderful friends and family that cared about me. "Thank you" just doesn't seem to be enough...

By Thursday, I was really beginning to feel the pain of my injuries. I was a pathetic mess to say the least. The nurses would give me pain medicine but it usually didn't help for long. I would moan and complain, *"Why is no one helping me?"* I had begun to hack up phlegm and was given what I affectionately called the "spit wand." This is a similar device to the one used in a dentist office to extract saliva.

It made a very annoying sound to everyone around me, especially Diane, but the "spit wand" and I became very close. Between being loopy from the pain medicine and my close relationship with my special friend, I was a reality TV show waiting to happen!

That same day, the General Manager of Silver Dollar City, John Baltes, came by to pay me a visit. Diane did her best to prepare him for what he was about to experience, although nothing could have prepared him for what he was about see. Apparently, I was acting a bit groggy from the pain medicine when he finally stepped into my intensive care room. The conversation went something like this....

"John..." I said very slow and slurred, almost drunk sounding, "What brings you out, John?"

"Well, to see you, Brian." John said.

"Oh, that's nice, John." I said with my "spit wand" firmly grasped in my hand. Then I asked him, "John, I just need to know...John, do I have a job?"

John and Diane cracked up laughing, but I was not deterred.

"No, John...I just want to know if I have a job?" I continued asking.

John smiled at me and said, "Well Brian, you can play anywhere on the park you want to."

"Well John, I just need a job," I said.

John chuckled.

"John...I'm writing a new song," I said.

"Really?" John said. "What's it about?"

I replied, "It's a sequel to Patsy Cline's big hit, 'I Fall To Pieces.'"

Laughter erupted and with a big grin on his face, John look at me with my "spit wand" in hand and said, "Yeah...I bet you could really 'spit' it out!"

I just looked up at him out of the corner of my eye, stuck my "spit wand" in my mouth and smiled!

By the time Friday afternoon rolled around, I was finally moved out of intensive care and into a regular hospital room. I now had a companion to my "spit wand": the morphine button! We all became fast friends.

I was also fitted with a new neck brace so that I could actually sit up in my bed. It felt good to be doing something besides staring at the ceiling and having my mind race in a million different directions. I would love to tell you that I was in good spirits and hopeful for a good outcome to my dilemma, but that would be a lie. I was scared, and quite frankly, I wanted to be left alone.

One thing I really hate about being in a hospital is the fact that nurses are always poking and prodding you with needles. They're running one test after another or waking you up to check your vitals. They had to do a urine test once and explained that they would have to place the urine on ice for at least twenty-four hours. I remember making a sarcastic joke about how that was a delicacy in Switzerland. (My apologies to the Swiss.)

Another thing about hospitals that I really don't care for is the food. I'm a very picky eater, so it's tough enough to find something I like. I was either complaining about the choices I had to choose from or that I had to eat anything at all. I was making things difficult on everyone because I felt that what had happened to me was totally unfair. *"Why isn't my arm getting better? What am I going to do if it doesn't? I'm a piano player..."*

After being in the hospital for a solid week, my parents and Diane made the decision to go home for a night. I know that they were a bit hesitant to leave me alone, but I was actually relieved. Don't get me wrong, I'm very grateful for the sacrifices they made to be there with me, but I needed time alone to think. I had to start figuring things out.

God... are you there? I know I've done some awful things in my life, but do I really deserve this? I've tried to be a good person and serve You the best I can. You know I'm sorry for divorcing Patty and I know it's not in Your plan for Diane and I to be living together... but did You have to let this happen? Didn't I lose enough when I lost my leg? Please God... not my arm too. Playing the piano means everything to me. I make my living as a piano player. I serve You as a piano player in a gospel group. Please God... I need a miracle.

I stared down at my lifeless arm and tried to will it to move, but nothing happened. Tears began to stream down my face. *I guess*

I'm just a royal screw up. I've made so many mistakes... Why me, God? I just want to be happy, that's all. Is that too much to ask? Where are You? I'm so sorry...

On Tuesday, January 25th, Diane's brother, Gary, had what he thought was a great idea. I had begun physical therapy and he thought bringing in a keyboard would be a good idea. I can remember trying to be polite but that was the *last* thing I wanted to see. *What good is a one armed piano player?* My depression was really starting to show. I wanted to hide from everyone but you can't do that when you're confined to a hospital bed. Someone is always coming in, whether it's well-meaning family and friends or doctors and nurses who are just trying to do their job.

Saturday, January 29, was a bittersweet day for me because Grandma Arnold was coming to see me for the first time since my accident. I loved my Grandma so much but the thought of seeing her cry was almost more than I could bear. She had *always* been my number one fan.

As a kid, every time she came to visit, she wanted to hear every new song I had learned. She even liked all the songs I wrote. I can remember every Christmas, all she ever wanted was a cassette tape of me playing the piano and singing, either by myself or with my family. All I could think about was that those days were over.

That thought was really beginning to set in. There was obviously no change in my left arm at all. The idea of it never moving again was becoming more and more of a reality. Of course, I put on my "happy" face for Grandma. I couldn't let her see how I was really feeling. She meant the world to me. Seeing her that day made me appreciate her all the more. Her simple smile that day was like a ray of sunlight into my ever-increasingly dark world. Grandma has since gone on to heaven and I miss her so much. To this day, when I perform I picture her sitting on the front row with that same smile on her face, beaming with pride, and I sing for her just as if she were still here.

It was truly an emotional day. Later that evening, I got an unexpected phone call from a man I had never met. His name was Tim Sheppard. Tim was a contemporary Christian singer from the '70s who I really admired. A friend of mine, Danny Byrd, had contacted him and told him about what I was going through and how I enjoyed his music.

To say I was humbled and surprised that he would call to encourage me would be an understatement. As I listened to him on the other end of the phone, I cried and began shaking. *How amazing is this?* Tim told me not give up, that God still had a plan for my life. Even though I wasn't sure if I really believed that, I knew it was a God-thing that he had called.

Even when we don't realize it, God is reaching out to us. We're never really alone. No matter how bleak the situation may seem, God really does have a plan for your life. You're never so broken or messed up, but what He can't put you back together. My friend and author of *90 Minutes In Heaven*, Don Piper, explains it like this: God can take mess of your life and turn it into a message. That message is always one of hope. Jesus says, *"I will never leave you, nor forsake you."* That is a promise you can count on.

"I can do all things thru Christ who strengthens me

I can do all things thru Christ who strengthens me

Though the world says I can't win

There's no way that I can lose

I can do all things thru Christ who strengthens me"

-Brian Arnold, Ted Burden, and Zane King
(From the song, "All Things Thru Christ")

"A journey of a thousand miles must begin with a single step."

                                    –Lao Tsu

"Casting all your care upon him; for he cares for you."

                                    1 Peter 5:7

Chapter Thirteen

A Long Road Gets Longer

On the last day of January 1994, I was moved to a room in the rehabilitation wing of the hospital, where I would remain until my release. It was here that I would meet some of most upbeat, motivational people on the planet... the exact kind I did NOT want to be around.

Most of the time when someone is depressed, they tend to be the thermostat in whatever room they're in. Their mood affects everyone else by bringing them down as well. This, however, was not the case with the folks in rehab. They were such annoying, happy people who could not wait to ruin my day.

All I really wanted to do was lay around and sulk, taking out my problems on those around me. I was still incredibly weak from everything I had been through. Every muscle in my body was sore, and even though it had only been a little over two weeks since the accident, I was like a baby trying to learn to walk again. It was all I could do just to stand up.

The name of my occupational therapist was Greg. He was definitely a realist. He was concerned with only the parts of my body that were, in his mind, going to work again. What this meant, was that I had to prepare for a life with the use of only one arm.

He began to instruct me on how to do things with one hand that I used to do with two. Simple things, like how to button my pants, how to tie my shoes, how to brush my teeth (try putting the toothpaste on the toothbrush...), and of course, how to tear the toilet paper off of the toilet roll. Try it sometime!

I can remember thinking, *If you want to teach me how to do something with one hand, teach me how to play the piano!* I had been a classically trained pianist. My whole identity had been woven in and around the piano. Somehow, learning to put on a shirt with one hand didn't hold much value in my crumbling world. Plus, the fact that Greg didn't hold any real hope for my arm recovering, added to my depression.

By the end of my third day in rehab, I was exhausted, both physically and emotionally. I began to cry even with people around. My thoughts were not focused on God somehow causing good to come out of all of this. The good thing would have been to not have to go through it at all. I just wanted to go home.

On Thursday, February 3, I finally got some good news. The rehab folks had decided that I was making good enough progress with my physical rehabilitation, that I could have a four-hour pass on Sunday to actually leave the hospital. All I wanted to do was go home. I had already spent more time in the hospital than in my new house.

When Sunday finally came around, I was so excited. It was no easy task for Diane, though. We were given instructions on being very careful. I still couldn't walk without a walker, so any kind of stairs was out. Just getting in and out of the car with a neck brace on was a challenge. *Don't bump my head…don't bump my head…*

Four hours is not a long time when you think about it, especially when an hour-and-a-half is spent in the car driving to and from. Diane did her best to drive slow and safe. Being safe was the easy part… she's a bit of an impatient driver. Once safely at our home, I was anxious to get inside. Having a neck brace on tends to make riding in a car a chore.

Diane told me to wait in the car while she got out to unlock the door of our home. When she came back to get me, she had a frazzled look on her face. I asked her what was wrong and she proceeded to tell me that she had accidentally left the key locked in the house. (Her house key was not on the same key ring as the car.) Fortunately, it only took about twenty minutes for a locksmith to get there and "break" us in.

It was good to be home, even if only for a short while. While being there, Diane trimmed my scraggly beard, gave me a haircut and placed the curls on the back of my head into a short ponytail. I didn't know it at the time, but this was the beginning of my long hair phase. The "mullet" was soon to appear! (Isn't it amazing when looking back, what we think was in style?) Before we knew it, our outing was over and I was being driven back to prison…I mean to the hospital.

The next day, I finally got some of the best news I had been given since entering the hospital over three weeks earlier. The doctor told me that if everything kept improving the way that it was supposed to, then I could possibly be going home for good by the end of the week. This was music to my ears and just the motivation I needed to work hard in physical therapy.

I was soon fitted with a sling to hold my left arm up and a brace for my hand to rest in. The sling actually wrapped around the back of my neck and looped under my right arm. I basically looked like I had a broken arm.

I was then introduced to nerve pain. I had phantom pains as a kid after I lost my leg (the kind of feelings like your leg is still there when it's not), but nothing like I was now experiencing.

About the best way I know to describe it is, imagine ripping your fingernails off one at a time, and then placing your hand in a vice and begin slowly tightening it down until the pain was completely unbearable. That is what nerve pain is to me.

At first, it would come and go, but as the days would turn into years, I could seldom go a single hour of my day without it. There's also really nothing you can take to stop the pain. About the only thing I could do when it got really bad was lay on my arm.

It was my constant companion and it took precedence over everything I did. I could be carrying on a conversation and have to stop mid-sentence and wait up to thirty seconds for it to release me from its grip. It would even cause my neck to draw down to where my chin would rest on my chest. Everything in my life was affected by it.

Today, I have been healed from the constant attack of nerve pain. Only on rare occasions, and usually when I'm sick, do I ever experience it anymore. I suffered for many long years and I truly can identify with those who still struggle with it. The Good News is that you don't have to! By His stripes I *HAVE* been healed!

Thursday, February 10, was my last day of therapy in the hospital. I was finally going home the next day. Thursday was memorable for a couple of different reasons. One, Grandma Arnold came by one last time to see me before I went home. It was good to see her and hear her tell me that everything would be all right.

Two, Diane had finally convinced Sue to bring my boys to the hospital to see me. I'll never forget the moment that they walked into my room. I was so excited to see them, as they were me, but for totally different reasons. They were almost six years old. I'm grateful to Diane for insisting that Sue bring them, and I'm also grateful that Sue set aside our differences long enough to do so.

The third reason that this day was so memorable is the conversation I had with my dad. I knew eventually that this day would come. It was the "talk" that was long overdue. Up until now, everyone had simply focused on my recovery, but now that I was being released from the hospital, he had a few things he needed to get off his chest.

Dad realized that even though I was going home, I was still in no condition to take care of myself and everyone, including his church people, knew it. Diane and I were engaged, but that was still not a reason for him to condone living together. As difficult as it may have been to say, he felt that he owed it to his convictions, and to God, to insist that we get married as soon as possible.

I knew in my heart, that what he was saying was correct. Too many people today live together out of convenience rather than commitment. I totally understand why God wants things done His way. The problem with this advice to me at that time in my life, is that I wasn't in *any* condition to make a long-term commitment and neither was Diane, for that matter.

Now before you think I'm condoning sin, let me remind you of all the emotional problems I was having. I had just lost the use of my arm. I hadn't even begun to process what this really meant for my life. *Would I ever play the piano again? I make my living as a piano player.* Also, I hadn't come to terms with my past, most of which Dad was oblivious to. Although his advice was Biblically correct, he was addressing the wrong problem and didn't even know it. Neither did I.

I was in such a vulnerable place emotionally, and I needed my dad's approval. I was tired of disappointing him and everyone else. I wanted God's approval too, so this felt like the only right thing to do. Once again, I didn't consult Him, I just thought I knew what He wanted me to do.

Diane was definitely not thrilled about the sudden rush to get married, but she had been getting some pressure applied from her family too. Her mother, Evelyn Kukal, had voiced concerns about our living conditions and the effect it might be having on Kelsey.

Diane had been thrust into the role of being my caretaker, so how could she possibly think straight for herself? She didn't want to abandon me in my time of need, but marrying me so abruptly was a bit scary. *Will Brian get the use of his arm back? Will he even be able to work and make a living? Will I be stuck taking care of him for the rest of my life?*

Another aspect to all of this was, Diane would have to give up her "big" wedding that had originally been planned for later that year on June 18th. She, unlike me, had never been married, and as any woman can tell you, it is a very big deal to have the wedding that you've been dreaming about since you were a little girl playing dress-up. *Do I really want to give up everything just to make other people happy? Do I still want to marry Brian after everything that's happened?*

These were real questions that needed time to be answered. Don't act so spiritual like the answers should have been so obvious, because they weren't. Too often, people rush to judgment without knowing all of the facts. *"The Bible says do this... so go do it right now."* That may be true, but I believe that God never intended for the Bible to just be a list of rules that Godly men and women enforced, but rather the Word to be applied out of a relationship with the Author.

Out of fear of disappointing anyone, and in the name of "doing the right thing," Diane and I agreed to get married as quickly and as quietly as possible. Eight days later on February 18, one week after I was released from the hospital, we were married in a small chapel in Eureka Springs, Arkansas, with only Kelsey and Diane's mother, Evelyn, in attendance.

Friday, February 11, was V-Day for me. After nearly dying and then spending twenty-seven days in St. John's Hospital, I was finally headed home for good...or at least I thought I was, but we'll get to that soon enough. I believe I could hear John Denver singing as we headed out of the parking lot...

"Country roads, take me home...to the place I belong..."

"Start by doing what's necessary; then do what's possible; and suddenly you are doing the impossible."

–Saint Francis of Assisi

"...I do believe; help me overcome my unbelief!"

Mark 9:24

Chapter Fourteen

Home Is Where The "Start" Is

Starting over is never really that much fun, but it's especially not when you didn't plan to. Here I was at the age of twenty-six and racked with emotional defeats. I had one leg, the use of one arm, recently divorced and now, newly married. I was unable to be a father to my own boys, yet I was now the father figure for a nine-year-old girl.

To say that I was depressed is probably a gross understatement. I can remember wanting to hide from everyone, including Diane. I was emotionally drained, yet reality was always right there on my doorstep.

I didn't have much time to just sit and sulk, I had to figure out what I was going to do. I had a house to pay for, a new family to support and daily incoming medical bills that were starting to pile up. When all else fails, economics to the rescue!

I'd love to say that it was my faith that spurred me into action, but that would be a lie. I had to figure out how I was going to make a living, and with Silver Dollar City opening back up in April, I had to do it quickly. I didn't want to be replaced. In fairness, neither Silver Dollar City nor Chosen Few ever once hinted of replacing me, but my fears were driving me. *Who wants a one-handed pianist?*

Keyboard sequencing was fairly popular in music back in the nineties. I realized that if I programmed a keyboard to play what my left hand should be playing, I could then play along with my right hand. My wallet quickly went into action and I used my credit card to purchase a Korg M1 Sequencer (approx. $2,000) and a Roland SB-55 Sound Brush.

I immediately went to work programming as much of the Chosen Few repertoire as I could. Believe it or not, the real challenge was getting the tempos of the songs correct. I don't know how many tracks I made that were either too fast or too slow. No matter how hard I tried, playing these songs in my bedroom never felt the same as when I was in front of an audience.

In spite of the urgency to get back to work, I still made time for the occasional pity party. *Why me?!* That's what I wanted to know. What I needed was counseling. I had more baggage to deal with than an international airport!

I didn't realize it of course, but I was still dragging around the image I had of myself as the little boy being made fun of for having a "wooden" leg. I was an outcast who felt that no one would ever love me the way I was. I was the rejected beau and the promiscuous son. I was the shameful father who had let his sons down. I was divorced—a death blow in most Christian circles.

And now…the one thing I had to feel proud about, had been ripped away from me…on my way to church of all things! *Thanks, God!*

I can remember sitting and staring at the piano, trying to will my left arm to work—but nothing. Mark Twain once said, *"The worst loneliness is not to be comfortable with yourself."* I can certainly understand what he was saying. I didn't like myself at all. Depression became an even closer friend to me during this time of my life.

I've often joked that I should have been sent to live on the Island of Misfit Toys. Remember this island from "Rudolph, The Red Nosed Reindeer"? King Moonracer was a winged lion that would fly around the world each night searching for defective and unwanted toys and bring them to live on the island. That was me…defective and feeling unwanted. King Moonracer never found me, and the dream of island living quickly faded as rehearsals for Silver Dollar City began.

America's Largest International Festival, World Fest, was first held in1994. Every year during April and May, performers and craftsmen from all over the globe converge on Silver Dollar City for what has grown to become the largest and one of the most renowned international festivals in the United States. This was the setting for my one- handed piano playing…unveiled.

By this point, I was still wearing a cervical neck collar and was unable to drive myself anywhere. My balance was slowly coming back and I was now using a cane to walk instead of a walker. Oh, the simple things we take for granted…

Silver Dollar City opened with a bang and Chosen Few was right in the middle of it all. The Gazebo Stage was our home during World

Fest, right in the heart of the square. Everyone entering the park had to walk right passed us as we performed. Obviously, our goal was singing and entertaining well enough that people would stop and stay for our show.

We used all of our quartet tricks to gain a crowd. Ashley would sing as high as he could on the tenor part, to which we would kid him about sounding like a woman. David would charm them with his Tennessee accent and southern charm, all the while spinning a tale that was sure to give any storyteller a run for his money. All Scott had to do was drop the bomb—code for "sing as low as possible!" Scott's bass voice would always draw a crowd.

Even with all of the busyness of the square...the sound of the blacksmith's hammer, the street troupe performers carrying on with guests, Popcorn Roy selling what else... popcorn(!), a myriad of activities happening all at once... Scott's booming bass voice would cut through it all and cause people to stop in their tracks. Then just for a surprise, he would show off his tremendous range and sing almost as high as Ashley.

It was almost like before my accident; except there were no flying hands coming up off of the piano as I played. There I sat with my left arm motionless in a sling and my neck in a brace, feeling like the odd man out. My sequenced tracks worked well but it wasn't the same for me. I certainly couldn't be as animated at the piano as I once was, but at least I was back to work.

It was good to be working again. Somehow just having a routine to follow, gave me a sense of accomplishment. John Baltes had kept his word and I had a job at Silver Dollar City. *Thanks John!*

My body grew stronger with each passing day and I was actually starting to feel better. It was soon time for a checkup with my neurologist, Mark Crabtree. I can remember how excited I was at the potential of no longer needing the cervical collar. I was looking forward to being able to drive myself again and gain some sense of independence back.

My appointment was scheduled for a day that I didn't have to work and Diane drove me to Springfield. Before I could see Mark, I had to have some x-rays done to assess my progress. My sense of anticipation was high. I was definitely leaving Mark's office without my cervical collar. *Who knows, maybe I'll drive us back home.* Boy, did I have a surprise coming!

After x-rays were completed, Diane and I sat in a patient room waiting for Mark to come in. When he finally came in my room, I could tell that something wasn't quite right by the look on his face. Mark proceeded to show us the x-rays and explain that my neck was not healing as he had originally hoped it would. Not only was it not healing, but my neck was actually way out of alignment and needed surgery to repair it. *You've got to be joking! I just got back to work!!*

Mark was insisting that I be immediately admitted into St. John's Hospital because any accidental bump could literally kill me. *This isn't happening!!*

"Mark," I said. "I can't just go right back into the hospital today. I'm supposed to work tomorrow."

"You really need to be under medical care right now. The slightest bump could cause your head to shift and you could die," Mark said.

"But I can't just go straight into the hospital, I have got to at least make plans for Chosen Few. I've got to help find somebody to replace me. How long am I going to be in this time?" I said.

"Probably a little over a week." Mark said. "We have to do anterior cervical spinal fusion surgery and chances are that you'll need to wear a halo brace for three or four months afterward."

By the time Mark got done explaining all that needed to be done to me, you could have knocked me over with a feather. First, the neck fusion:

To achieve a spinal fusion, a bone graft (from my hip) is used to promote two bones growing together into one. In this case, bone will grow into and around the bone graft and incorporate the graft bone as its own. This process creates one continuous bone surface and eliminates motion at the fused joint.

Second, the halo brace:

First developed by Dr. Vernon L. Nickel at Rancho Los Amigos National Rehabilitation Center in 1955, the halo brace (also known as a halo ring, halo vest or halo crown) is a cervical thoracic orthosis brace used to immobilize the cervical spine, usually following fracture. The halo brace allows the least cervical motion of all cervical braces currently in use.

It is ring-shaped, made up of metal, and goes around your head. It is secured directly into your skull with four metal pins. The brace is then attached to a vest by four metal bars that the patient must wear to help bear the brace's weight. Barbaric-sounding, isn't it?

The surgery didn't scare me near as much as the sound of the halo brace! Mark told me that you are awake when the brace is put on. *AWAKE?!! Put me out and don't wake me up until it comes off!*

After pleading my case and getting some stern warnings on being careful, Mark allowed me to go home and make preparations. Needless to say, I didn't get to drive home. I'm not sure that even a lot was said as Diane drove back toward Branson. *Could it get any worse?*

Once again, Chosen Few and Silver Dollar City were incredibly gracious to my family and me. They stood behind me every step of the way. Even after the surgery, when I was looking like some kind of malfunctioning robot, I was welcomed back to work. I can never repay the kindness that I was shone during this dark period of my life.

The night that I checked back into the hospital was probably my lowest point. I remember lying in bed with my head in traction, crying in the dark. Everything seemed to be crumbling beneath me. Just when I thought that things were going to level out... BAM! Another setback. (BAM—Brian Arnold Ministries; shameless plug, I know!)

How many times can one person get knocked down and still be expected to get back up? God seemed to be a million miles away. I wasn't sure that I was even a blip on His radar. My failures and heartaches were beginning to be too many to count.

A couple of days after the neck fusion surgery, the doctors came in to put on my halo brace. I can still remember the sound of my skull crunching as the metal screw pins turned inward. All I could do was cry...

True to his word, Mark released me from the hospital a week later. Diane had to work that day, so Ashley agreed to pick me up and take me home. As he walked into my room that day to get me, he greeted me.

"Hi Brian. You're looking good!" Ashley said.

I replied, "That's RoboCop to you!"

Even with my best friend, I couldn't open up and tell how I was really feeling. At this point, I'm not sure if I really knew myself. I was numb.

Looking at myself in a mirror left much to be desired. I was truly a horrific sight to behold. I looked on the outside like I felt on the inside. Broken and messed up. How could I face anyone? I couldn't dress myself and besides, nothing fit around the vest of the halo brace unless it was velcroed. That is definitely hard to do with a paralyzed arm. I didn't feel like an entertainer, a gospel singer, a newlywed or even much like a man. *What could God possibly do with me?*

My first day back to work at Silver Dollar City was interesting to say the least. I was an attraction all on my own. Everyone stopped and stared at me. I couldn't help but draw attention to myself because of the way I looked. People would look at me and wince in pain. But the funniest thing was when they saw me walk toward the stage and start playing the piano and singing. They would be like... *No way!*

Suddenly everyone wanted to know what had happened to me. I reluctantly began to share about my accident with people as they would ask and eventually, the guys in Chosen Few insisted that I share my story from the stage. People came out of the woodwork to talk to me. Some shared stories of friends or family that had worn a halo brace, and some just wanted to thank me for being an inspiration to them. *An inspiration? Me? How could I possibly inspire anyone?*

Day after day and show after show, people thanked me for hanging in there and not quitting. Before my three-month halo sentence was up, Silver Dollar City had placed Chosen Few inside the Riverfront Playhouse to do shows, and in every one of them I shared my story. The Riverfront Playhouse was an air-conditioned, 700-seat venue and I was extremely grateful to be inside out of the one-hundred-plus-degree weather.

God slowly began to melt my heart. He said to me, *"I don't need your abilities. I just want your availability. I'm not finished with you yet!"* Romans 8:28 states, "And we know that all things work together for good to them that love God, to them who are the called according to his purpose."

God has the unique ability to win with any hand He is dealt. What an amazing promise! The real problem is us trusting in His goodness. Too often we blame God for the tragedies that happen to us. There's even a faction of folks in the religious community that actually believe God causes things like what happened to me. How absurd is that?

Jesus said, *"The thief comes to steal, kill and destroy..."* I know who my enemy is and it's NOT God! All throughout my life, God has been reaching toward me with His hands of love, even when I wasn't looking or I had my back turned against Him.

It took awhile for me to see it, but once my eyes were truly opened, all I could see was God's goodness. Everywhere I look, I see Him. If only the rest of the world would open their eyes...*The Kingdom of Heaven is at hand!*

A few years later while praying for a miracle, God showed me an important lesson. I was bartering with God, saying things like, *"If you'll give me the use of my arm back, I promise to do a real good job on Oprah Winfrey's show!"* I wanted something along the lines of Moses parting the Red Sea.

I was sitting on my back deck when God directed my attention through the sliding glass door of my home. There on the floor was my youngest daughter, Kerrigan. She was playing and totally unaware that I was watching her. God said something important to me that night that has stuck with me. I even put it in a song I wrote. He said, *"Don't get so caught up looking for the 'big' things, that you overlook all of the 'little' things I place in your life every day to show you how much I love you."*

That's not to say that God doesn't still perform miracles, because He does. It doesn't mean don't pursue your healing or the miracle you need either. But it does mean, God is *ALWAYS* there, no matter what you are going through, even when you've been run over by a lawnmower and a semi-trailer.

"It's the little things that I can't live without

It's more than just miracles God is all about

It's the little things that hold my life together

I don't need a parting sea

Everyday I wake up, I ask God for more of the little things."

–Brian Arnold
(From the song "The Little Things")

"Victory at all costs, victory in spite of all terror, victory however long and hard the road may be; for without victory there is no survival."

–Sir Winston Churchill

For everyone born of God overcomes the world. This is the victory that has overcome the world, even our faith.

1 John 5:4

Chapter Fifteen

From Victim to Victory

A lot has happened in my life since 1994, some great things and some not so great things. I'd love to say, *"And we all lived happily ever after,"* but life is a journey of ups and downs. Just when I think I've got it all figured out, I'm hit by another curveball. The fact is, life isn't easy! We have an enemy roaming to and fro, seeking whom he may devour. He is out to steal, kill and destroy us. The sooner you figure out that you're in a war, the better.

Along the way, I have had some great victories. One of which was gaining custody of my boys, Austin and Justin. They came to live with us at the age of twelve. I finally got to know more than just their names.

Raising them through their teenage years was a challenge though, not to mention them dealing with their own identity crises. I sure could have used some help from Sherwood Schwartz because we were definitely not the Brady Bunch. Our problems did not get solved in thirty minutes or less. Some battles in life are longer, with wounds that are deeper.

Chosen Few became a highly successful regional quartet. David left the group and was replaced by Ashley's younger brother, Casey. This is when we really hit our stride. We signed a major record deal with Journey Records in Nashville, Tennessee, and began making some of our best recordings. Thanks to Zane King, we recorded many of my songs, including "The Little Things," which had moderate success nationally.

We went on to headline the 4,000-seat outdoor Echo Hollow amphitheater at Silver Dollar City for several years, and in 2001, our show was named "Branson's Show Of The Year." We left Branson at the end of that year and entered into a full-time traveling ministry. We were blessed to sing and minister all over the United States, with even a mission trip to Nicaragua.

Chosen Few was going gang-busters, but like many groups, the members eventually begin to be involved in solo endeavors. Recently I read an interview with guitar legend Robbie Robertson, in which he detailed his version of the Band's break-up (and this version most assuredly differs from Levon Helm's!). He simply said the individual members had other things to do.

I think that's where I came to be with Chosen Few. We remain wonderful friends, and those guys have no greater admirer than me. *Thanks Ashley, Casey and Scott! I love you guys!! You too Dan!* (Dan Lyming was our road manager, bus driver, sound technician and friend.)

In 2005, I followed in my father's footsteps. I was licensed and ordained as a minister of the Gospel by Pastor Tim Brooks and

Christian Ministries Church in Hot Springs, Arkansas. Tim's approach to God's Word has had a dramatic effect on my ministry and me. He's applied life all the way and I owe him a great deal. This was the beginning of my solo ministry.

Also in 2005, I met my dearest friend in the world, Bob Barnes. I had purchased a 1997 Winnebago Adventurer motorhome and was in need of assistance. I knew nothing about motorhomes except that they were a comfortable way to travel.

I happened to be speaking at my home church, First Baptist Church in Kimberling City, Missouri, and mentioned that if anyone knew anything about motorhomes, I could use their help. Bob and his wife, Judy, were fairly new to the church but he came to my rescue. He introduced himself and gave me a crash course on all of the pertinent information I would need to operate such a vehicle.

Almost a year later, I met Bob again in an automotive repair shop. He began to share the wonderful experiences he had in Brazil with Randy Clark's ministry, Global Awakening. I was mesmerized by the stories of God's power in action. From that point on, Bob and I became best of friends. He is my armor-bearer, my prayer partner and an integral part of my ministry today. *Thanks Bob! Let's keep looking for the "suddenlies"!*

In 2006, I hooked up with my buddy, Zane King again, but this time instead of signing a record deal, I was blessed to become an Artist/Speaker with Compassion International.

Founded by the Rev. Everett Swanson in 1952, Compassion began providing Korean War orphans with food, shelter, education and health care, as well as Christian training.

Compassion exists as a Christian child advocacy ministry that releases children from spiritual, economic, social and physical poverty and enables them to become responsible, fulfilled Christian adults. Today, Compassion helps more than one million children in 26 countries. I have personally been to Bolivia and Guatemala to see firsthand the ministry of Compassion. What a tremendous privilege it is to partner with such an amazing organization.

2006 was also a challenging year for my marriage. I had still not fully come to terms with everything that had happened in my life and it all came boiling to a head with Diane. We had grown very distant and bitter over everything, and neither of us really knew how to handle our "stuff," let alone each other.

At one point, I decided that I just needed a clean start. It was after an intense, heated argument that I decided to move out. To make matters worse, I immediately entered into a relationship with someone else. I fell into a familiar trap. What was it Einstein said?

After a year-long separation, we decided to give it another try. Each day continues to be a new adventure, but hopefully we are learning to approach things in a more honest way. Free will is a tricky thing. I've learned that dealing with my "stuff" first is the key. I'll never be able to change anybody but me, and I can't do that alone. God is constantly weaving a tapestry that each of us must be a willing part of. I owe a tremendous debt of gratitude to some guys who never gave up on me. *Thanks Clif, Dennis, Joe, Randy and Todd.*

As I look back at my marriage to Diane, I'm not sure that I have ever really thanked her for the sacrifices she has made. She has been the one who has mowed the yard, changed the diapers, washed the dishes, hammered the nails and screwed the screws…you get the picture. *Thank you, Diane...You most certainly are an angel worthy of Heaven!*

In 2007, I was blessed to meet a wonderful older friend by the name of Betty Hastings. Betty came to one of my concerts one night in middle Tennessee, and afterwards, offered her assistance to my ministry. She was a twice-widowed pastor's wife, looking for a way to serve the Lord in her twilight years. Betty has more energy than any three teenagers you might know. She wasn't looking for a rocking chair to settle into and start waiting to go to Heaven...oh no!

Betty went to work right away as my ministry coordinator, which is just a fancy title for the person who handles "everything." She does it all to the glory of God and I'm forever in her debt. *Thank you Betty! I love you!!*

Betty also began to open doors for me to help with foster parent organizations around the country. Being a former foster child and foster parent herself, she understood better than most, the needs of our children here locally in the United States. Many of these children are struggling with their own identity crisis, so she went to work getting me opportunities to speak to these kids. I've been blessed to work with state and private organizations in Alabama, Georgia, Louisiana, Minnesota, Missouri, North Carolina and Tennessee.

In 2009, I met two wonderful men in Mountain City, Tennessee, Bill Icenhour and Sterling Carroll, who helped open an amazing door for me. Bill and his wife, Phyllis, own a wonderful cabin up on one of the tallest mountains in east Tennessee. This place is about as close to Heaven as one can get here on Earth. They decided to have a get together with their friends one night, and invited me to sing and speak to them.

Sterling was in attendance that night and after hearing my story, decided that Franklin Graham needed to hear it as well. Franklin is the son of Billy Graham, and the president and CEO of both the Billy Graham Evangelistic Association and the international Christian relief organization, Samaritan's Purse. I honestly passed it off as a nice gesture, but didn't give much thought to it actually happening. True to his word, Sterling contacted his friend, Franklin, and told him, *"You've got to hear Brian's story!"*

A couple of months later, I was asked to come to Boone, North Carolina and share my story with Franklin Graham and the employees of Samaritan's Purse. What an honor it was to meet Franklin and to pray with him. Since then, I have been to Ecuador to help pass out shoeboxes with Operation Christmas Child, a global Christmas gift exchange project operated by Samaritan's Purse. I was also asked to be a keynote speaker at three national volunteer conferences hosted by this incredible ministry. *Thank you Bill and Sterling, and Samaritan's Purse!*

Most recently, I've been asked to host my own weekly television program on TCT (Total Christian Television—Directv Channel 377). TCT is recognized as a leader in inspirational television and worldwide, and reaches potentially 1.5 billion viewers.

This wonderful opportunity came about through my association with Don Enz. Don and I had gone to church together, and I knew that he had connections because of his work in the Christian publishing field. Don contacted his good friend, Judy Church, and the rest as they say, is history! Don is a great friend and has gone on to serve as my personal manager. *Thanks Don and Judy!*

My program is called...what else, *"From Victim to Victory."* The focus of my program is teaching others to become an overcomer. I interview people from all walks of life about the different challenges they have faced, and how they have gone from living the life of a victim, to living a life of victory.

So I guess that brings me full circle, to the reason I wrote this book. Although my life sounds like a combination of Opie Taylor and a soap opera, I can tell you without question that almost every trial we face in life ultimately comes down to a question of our identity.

Who am I really? Do I really have any value?

And if it's not about our identity, then it's about God's integrity.

Why would a good God let bad things happen?

God doesn't mean EVERYTHING He says, does He?

This is an age-old problem. It goes all the way back to Adam and Eve in the Garden of Eden. God says, *"Let Us create man in Our own image and in Our own likeness."*

What was God saying to them? *"We made you to be like Us!"*

God gave Adam and Eve their identity from the very beginning. Then along comes the enemy and what does he say?

"If you really want to be like God..." Whoa! The conversation should have stopped right there. Adam and Eve should have said, *"We ARE like God. He said so already!"*

But they didn't say that. The enemy said, *"If you really want to be like God, eat the fruit of that tree."*

There it was...the seed of doubt was planted in the minds of Adam and Eve. They began to question their identity, and the integrity of God. The enemy convinced them that they needed to *do something* to be like God. In this case, eat the fruit from the tree of the knowledge of good and evil.

The reality was that Adam and Eve didn't need to do anything to be like God because they already were.

But that seed of doubt began to grow in their hearts and we all know what happened next. They tried to *do something* to be like God. My friends, that is the definition of religion. The fall of mankind was all about questioning our identity and God's integrity. It has been going on ever since.

So how do we win this battle? By looking to Jesus as our example. First, remember that Jesus was just a man like you and I. He was not *super*-Jesus. He came to show us what a man in right relationship with the Father could accomplish.

Let's look at what happened after Jesus' baptism. The heavens open, a dove descends and a voice is heard saying, *"This is My beloved Son, in whom I am well pleased."*

Jesus is then led into the wilderness, where He is tempted by the enemy. The devil says, *"If you're really the Son of God..."* Does that sound remotely familiar?

"If you're really the Son of God, turn these stones into bread." Or in other words, *"If you're really the Son of God, DO SOMETHING to prove it!"*

This is the same temptation that was used in the Garden of Eden. The enemy wanted Jesus to question His identity and His Father's integrity. How did Jesus defeat the devil?

Here's our example:

Jesus said, *"It is written..."*

What was He saying? *"My Father has already spoken on the matter and here is what He said."*

Jesus defeated the devil by believing what His Father had already said about Him. He didn't question His identity. He believed in the goodness of His Father.

Let these words sink into the core of your being.

God says, *"You are my son! You are my daughter! I am PLEASED with you!"*

If Jesus is the Lord of your life, then nothing else needs to be done. Our righteousness is nothing but filthy rags anyway! It's the righteousness of Jesus that sets us free. We can NEVER be good enough to be like God. We can NEVER do enough "good things" to be like God. It's only through Jesus. He is our identity!

I had to get to the point where I quit looking in the mirror to see who I was. I had to quit watching TV to see who I needed to be like or dress like. My friends couldn't tell me who I was, and neither could my family. Only God could speak to my soul and say, *"You are my son! I am PLEASED with you. You are more than a conqueror! You are fearfully and wonderfully made. You can do ALL THINGS through Jesus who strengthens you!"*

And to believe your true identity means you have to believe in the goodness of God. God's integrity is at stake here. The enemy wants you to think that God doesn't really care about you.

"If God really cares, then why do bad things happen to good people?"

There are a number of ways to answer this question, so I'll give it my best.

God gave us free will from the very beginning. This was truly an amazing gift. He gave us the ability to make our own choices. His gift came with instructions though, a list of do's and don'ts. The enemy has convinced us that this list is a bad thing from an angry taskmaster who simply doesn't want us to have fun.

First, God does not lie. Numbers 23:19 says, *"God is not human, that he should lie, not a human being, that he should change his mind. Does he speak and then not act? Does he promise and not fulfill?"*

Second, we must remember that our enemy *is* a liar. The Bible calls him the "father of lies". John 8:44 states, *"He was a murderer from the beginning, not holding to the truth, for there is no truth in him. When he lies, he speaks his native language, for he is a liar and the father of lies."*

God's list of do's and don'ts was really a list of causes and effects. If you do this, this will happen. If you don't do this, this won't happen. Everything God told us was out of love, not domination. It was also the truth.

With free will came dominion of the earth. Genesis 1:28 says, *"And God blessed them, and God said unto them, Be fruitful, and* multiply, and replenish the earth, and subdue it: and have dominion over the fish of the sea, and over the fowl of the air, and over every living thing that moveth upon the earth."

The word dominion means "control or the exercise of control; sovereignty: A territory or sphere of influence or control; a realm."

Are you starting to see the picture? God, out of His great love for us, gave us free will to make our own choices, and gave us the earth as our place to reign. The enemy has somehow convinced us that God is responsible for everything, when in reality it is our responsibility!

The devil deceived and cheated us out of our inheritance and then has the gall to say that it is God's fault. This needs to make you angry! Now, we're mad at God for being so loving toward us and blaming Him for the condition our world is in.

Jesus said in John 10:10, "The thief (our enemy) comes to steal, kill and destroy..." The fact is, the devil is jealous of you and I. He wants what you and I have, and he is out to destroy us at all costs and with whatever means necessary—even lawnmowers and semi-trucks!

He starts when we're young, planting seeds of doubt. He twists and turns everything, spinning his lies to make you believe that God sends tragedy, sickness and disease to teach us lessons in patience and humility. THIS IS WRONG!!!

Bill Johnson puts it like this: "If I did something like this to my own child, I would be arrested for child abuse!"

Quit blaming God for everything bad that happens and start being who you were created to be. 1 Peter 2:9 says, "But you are a *chosen people, a royal priesthood, a holy nation, God's special possession, that you may declare the praises of Him who called you out of darkness into His wonderful light."*

Jesus said, *"I come so that you can have life, and have it more abundantly."*

God has put everything in place that we need, in order to take back dominion over the earth. Jesus did it *all* at the cross. The curse was reversed and our true identity was restored. Don't live your life as a victim any longer!

Franklin Graham says it like this: *"No matter what storm you face, you need to know that God loves you. He has not abandoned you."*

Romans 8:28 states, *"And we know that all things work together for good to them that love God, to them who are the called according to his purpose."*

Oh my friend, hear me when I say... *"With Jesus...you're somebody special!"*

Today, I live my life in victory. I refuse to give up any more ground to my enemy. He has taken more than enough from me already. I have been awakened to who I really am. I am a son of the most high God and He thinks I'm special!

When my enemy tells me I can't, I call him a liar and announce to him that, *"I can...I can do ALL THINGS through Christ who strengthens me."*

Recently, I've been pressing in even more to become who God says I really am. I'm blessed to have a band of brothers who continue to challenge me to new heights. *Thanks Dan R., Dan L., Jerry, and Pat.*

In Mark 16:17-18, Jesus says something very bold: *"And these signs will accompany those who believe: In my name they will drive out demons; they will speak in new tongues; they will pick up snakes with their hands; and when they drink deadly poison, it will not hurt them at all;* **they will place their hands on sick people, and they will get well**." (Emphasis added)

He also said in John 14:12, *"Verily, verily, I say unto you, He that believeth on me, the works that I do shall he do also; and greater works than these shall he do; because I go unto my Father."*

This is all about taking dominion over the enemy and being who God created us to be. I'll share one last story in closing.

Not long ago, I was speaking in a church in McEwen, Tennessee. At the end of the service, a sixteen-year old boy named Kenneth came forward for prayer. He was complaining about pain in his eye.

He explained how he had been weed-eating when he hit a piece of barb-wire that suddenly landed in his eye. They had to surgically remove the barbed wire and Kenneth was left with a permanent hole in his eye. He had been given eye drops to control the swelling of his eye, yet he still had unbearable pain.

I found myself at a crossroad. *Who am I really?*

The enemy immediately began telling me that there was no way I could help this boy, besides if anybody needed a miracle it was me.

I had a choice to make. Who was I going to believe?

Would I believe God when He said, *"By the stripes of Jesus you HAVE been healed"*?

Or would I look at myself and say, *"How could God possibly use me?"*

I chose to be obedient to what God had spoken. I believe that God is good and that we have been charged with taking back dominion from our enemy.

I laid my hand on Kenneth's eye and remembered what Jesus taught in the Lord's Prayer. *The Father's will MUST be done on earth as it is in Heaven! There is no pain in Heaven!*

I didn't need to pray about what the Father's will was, because I already knew what He desired, what He already paid for with Jesus on the cross.

I took authority over the pain, cursed it and commanded it to go. I then released divine healing over Kenneth's eye.

Guess what happened? Nothing.

I could have given up and gone home feeling sorry for myself. I could have listened to my enemy and thought to myself, *"How foolish of me. I'm nobody!"*

I could have decided at that moment to once again be a victim, but I didn't. I told Kenneth to keep believing for what God promised.

Two weeks later, I received a phone call from Kenneth. He was unusually excited. He began to tell me about going to a new eye doctor. You see, Kenneth is a foster child and they get moved to different doctors from time to time.

The eye doctor had examined Kenneth's eye and couldn't find a hole anywhere! The doctor even asked him which eye had been hurt. Not only was the hole gone, but his vision was now 20/20. No more eye drops were necessary and there was no longer any pain.

This is only the beginning of the stories I could tell you. Why would God use a one-legged, one-armed piano player to heal anyone? Because God can win with any hand He is dealt. He didn't need my ability, just my availability.

Again, my friend Don Piper says it like this: God takes the mess of our lives and turns it into a message to share.

What about my healing? Some things come in seed form. In I Corinthians 3:6 Paul says, *"I have planted, Apollos watered; but God gave the increase."* You don't plant a tomato seed in the ground and the next day eat tomatoes. It takes time and caring for the seed that has been planted.

God is better than you think He is! God is GOOD!

My message is hope. You have hope in Jesus. Find your true identity in Him and believe in the goodness of God.

Wherever you are in your life—and you can now see that I speak from personal experience—if you are in a valley, set your eyes on that mountaintop, and keep stepping up with your hand in Jesus' hand. He will not leave you.

Go from victim…to victory!

"The dates you see upon that stone, the beginning and the end

They don't start to tell the story how you spend your life my friend

It's that little line between the years not our worth in land or cash

The only thing that counts down here is how we spend the dash"

—Brian Arnold and Charles Isbell
(From the song "How We Spend The Dash")

Also follow Brian on...
   www.brianarnoldministries.com
   www.bransonmoroadshow.com
   www.facebook.com/brianarnold67
   www.twitter.com/brianarnold67
   www.youtube.com/user/natkingfan

Watch Brian's weekly tv show on TCT (Directv #377) Sunday nights at 7:30 p.m. (EST) 6:30 p.m. (CST) or www.tct.tv

Want to schedule Brian for an event?
   BRIAN ARNOLD MINISTRIES
   40 Foust Lane
   Hollow Rock, Tennessee 38342
   888-391-5247

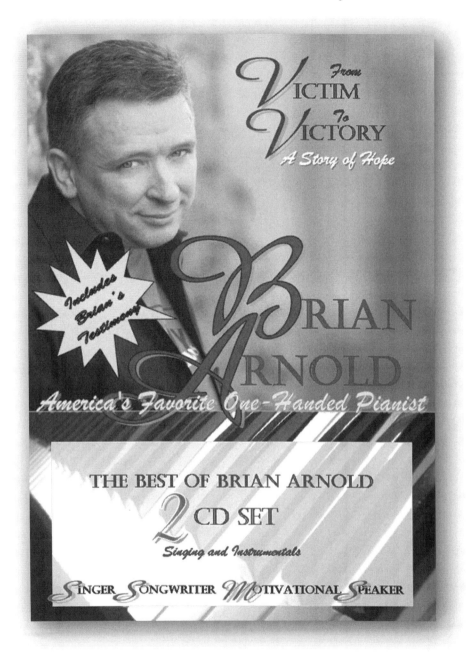

Order your copy today of
The Best of Brian Arnold.

This two CD set includes over 30 of Brian's
most requested songs as well as his testimony.

Made in the USA
Middletown, DE
23 May 2022

66093782R00128